CREATE
CALM

The Professionals Guide to Overcoming Anxiety from the Inside Out

DR. KATIE THOMSON AITKEN ND

ISBN: 978-1-7772857-0-8

DOWNLOAD THE AUDIOBOOK FREE!

READ THIS FIRST

Just to say thank you for buying my book, I would like to give you the Audiobook version 100% FREE!

TO DOWNLOAD GO TO:

www.katiethomsonaitken.com/createcalm-audiobook

TAKE ACTION WHILE READING THIS BOOK

Tranquil Minds Workbook

Designed for use in my clinical practice I'm sharing the same booklet I give my patients in private practice with you!

The worksheets inside it will give you the space to TAKE ACTION as you read this book!

GET YOUR FREE WORKBOOK:

www.katiethomsonaitken.com/tranquilmindsworkbook

Table of Contents

INTRODUCTION

Chapter One
LETTER TO THE READER

Dear Reader,

You probably picked up this book because there is a serious lack of chill in your life right now. You are anxious and overwhelmed. I started this book in the Fall of 2019, and this was already true for many people then.

Modern life has the stressors of managing kids, parents, and work. Not to mention managing a household and possibly even making time for friends, hobbies, and health!

As I finish writing, we are in the Spring of 2020. There is a global pandemic. If the world was anxious before (and to be clear, it was), our collective anxiety is chart-topping right now.

As anxious as things seem, they can be changed. Anxiety is not a fact. It is a response. It is not permanent; it is a transient state.

You can be less anxious and stressed out. You can have more calm in your life. I can help and guide you.

In fact, that is what I designed this book to do: walk you step by step into a more peaceful and calm version of this life.

I will share with you the methodology I use to treat anxiety and stress in my clinical practice with my patients. I developed this program with a combination of evidence-based recommendations and my insights from clinical experience as a practitioner over the past five years.

While I will offer my very best professional, authoritative guidance and support, let me also take a moment to say:

Ahem.

YOU CAN DO THIS!!

I BELIEVE IN YOU!!

I cannot do it for you.

Only you can do this.

And I hope you do. You deserve some peace in your mind and in your life.

You deserve to have the skills to set yourself up for less anxious days and to turn those days around when you are anxious without having to shut yourself off totally.

Yes, it is going to be work. If you aren't into that, I would just pass this book off to a friend or pick it up next year when you are ready to make some changes. I'm sorry if that sounds a bit harsh, but you do need to be prepared to do some work to make the most out of this book. Reading it alone will not change your life.

> **Anxiety is not a fact.**
> **It is a response.**
> **It is not permanent;**
> **it is a transient state.**

I hope you do read this book and I hope you try the suggestions within it. You may want a pen and notebook, or a dedicated note on your smartphone to do the work as you read along. On average, my patients reduce their standardized anxiety scores by half as a result of following this methodology. Such massive results showcase the power of naturopathic medicine[1].

A quick note on that: I am a naturopathic doctor, but I'm not your naturopathic doctor. This book is full of advice - dare I say it - great advice. But it's not medical advice. Remember that you might need your own medical/naturopathic doctor or your own therapist to work through some of these things in an individualized way.

All that being said, You can create a life on your own terms that will bring you meaning and joy and not fear and anxiety.

Let's get started.

Dr. Katie

[1] Breed, C., & Bereznay, C. (2017). Treatment of Depression and Anxiety by Naturopathic Physicians: An Observational Study of Naturopathic Medicine Within an Integrated Multidisciplinary Community Health Center. Journal of alternative and complementary medicine (New York, N.Y.), 23(5), 348–354. https://doi.org/10.1089/acm.2016.0232

Chapter Two

BOUNDARIES

I WAS THIRTEEN WHEN I WROTE MY FIRST BUCKET LIST. IT WAS QUITE LONG, and I'm sure I still have it somewhere. On it, I had a list of all kinds of things I wanted for my life. Professional goals like 'become a naturopathic doctor.' Personal goals like 'be a mom.' Fun goals like 'dye my hair red and play Titania in an actual performance of A Midsummer's Night Dream.'

I've accomplished a lot of these things. Some, I've let go because I honestly no longer want them. Others I'm still striving for.

Regardless of whether I've done them or not, I needed to set up boundaries to make them happen.

I didn't say "I want to write a book" for years and then spontaneously have a manuscript appear one day on my laptop.

I first had to decide to do it. I mean, really decide to do it and fully commit myself.

Then, I had to create the structure so that I could follow through with my goal of writing this book for you. This structure is what I call boundaries, and you are going to need it too.

It's incredibly important we cover this first, right now. Throughout this book, there are many things I recommend based on my research and clinical experience that you can change in your life to create more peace and tranquillity and less stress and anxiety. Some of these things you will be able to change in a heartbeat. I'll say "give yourself 5 minutes to breathe," and you'll set a phone alarm for 9 pm, take some breathing time every evening, and be done with it.

But some things are going to be harder. I'll suggest something that you already know you *should* be doing or even want to do! Yet, the 'how' eludes you. This boundaries exercise is the system to discover:

→   Your true reason for wanting to do something
→   What stops you from doing it
→   The infrastructure you need to put in place to get out of your own way

We need boundaries. They let us be fully present as ourselves.

Why You Need Boundaries

Boundaries are what lets yeses really mean yes. If we agree to something, and we don't mean it, then our yeses don't mean anything. If you do that to avoid the discomfort of the present 'no', then you build a life of discomfort. Following this, it's easy to end up with a metaphorical plate full of things that we said 'yes' to just because we didn't know how to say 'no.' Constant discomfort as a direct result of avoiding temporary discomfort. Anxiety. Setting boundaries in advance gives us a framework with which to say 'no,' and, when you need it, a reason to say 'no.'

I know sometimes it can seem like a challenge to say 'no' to something if you don't have a "good reason" for it. You may be thinking it's not kind to say 'no' if it's something you are capable of doing, especially if you value kindness and generosity. But not wanting to say 'no' in such a circumstance is a good reason. Needing to put your focus somewhere else is a good reason. First, you need to be kind and generous to yourself.

It also doesn't work very well in the long term to say 'no' to something you want to say yes to because you "should." Exercising, "so I don't gain weight," is a weak boundary built on a "no." This boundary sounds like it's internally focused, but in fact, it's built on avoiding something. Let me explain.

Say you see your neighbour jogging in the morning. You may think "how peaceful does that look, I'd love to go for a jog in the morning, but I've got too many emails, and I've got to make sure my child is awake before I head into the office." That's a 'yes' motivation. You want to run, but you have important things that prevent you from doing that right now. The work on boundaries in this situation is to carve out the time for a morning jog so that you are living a life aligned with your authentic desires.

But many people see their neighbour's morning jog and think, "There goes Mr. Iron Man." this type of judgement has nothing to do with the behaviour of our neighbour and everything to do with our own critical self-judgement. The proof of this is in the follow-up thought, "I should go for a run." Let's set aside for a moment whether or not you objectively should go for a run. Using shame, guilt, and judgement as a motivator to change your habits doesn't work well in the long term - even if it has worked for you in the past.

What works much better is moving TOWARD the life you want, rather than trying to run AWAY from something you don't want. The first thing that you need to do is just figuring out what you want. This is, in all honesty, probably the hardest work of the whole chapter - maybe even this entire book.

To have effective boundaries, we first need to identify what we want. That lets us create boundaries around what we don't want.

What do you want?

What do you want more of in your life? What's going to make your heart sing? When you look back at your week, what makes you think, "I wish I had more time doing this?" What is that? Is it, "I didn't have enough time to exercise?" Is it "I didn't spend quality time with my kids when I was with them?" Is it "I did not have enough great conversations with my spouse," is it "I did not have enough great sex with my spouse?" I'll say it one more time - what is it that you want? Now write that thing down, whatever it may be.

Make a list of what you love in your current life. The things you already have that you know your younger self would be pinching themselves in disbelief at the knowledge it is now yours. Anything that delights you – it goes on the list.

Now start adding the things you sometimes do and wish you did more. Include things that made younger versions of yourself happy. Include things that future versions of you would be super proud of you for doing. Think of your work, family, and community. Are there any charities or projects you wish you were more involved in? Think about those.

Avoid putting things you hate on this list. It's easy to imagine future you as an evolved person who enjoys literature or golfing more than current you – and, while that's possible - unless your child self always dreamed of being a great golfer - leave it off the list in favour of things you actually like.

Overall this list should only contain things that help you bring your best version of yourself into this world because that is the version you deserve. That is the version your kids and your family deserve. That is the version that you want to be at work. Frankly, that is the version that is going to lift up the vibration of this planet. Sorry to get a little woo-woo there. It's just, that is the version that we all need you to be. We all need for you to be the best, highest version of yourself as often as possible. And so write down what you want so that you can make that happen.

Take Action 🖉

Write down your list of what you want. Write down each item in the present tense – regardless of whether you currently have that thing or are that thing. For example, write, "I am strong and active," even if you currently think something more like, "I'm a lazy couch potato who should work out more." If you do think like this, that's another matter. You are not alone. We will address this crappy self-talk later.

What's in the Way

Now that you are clear about what you want, it's time to get into why you don't have that thing right now. Whether it is eating more vegetables or owning a cottage on the lake, things are stopping you from having and doing what would bring joy and contentment to your life.

Look at your list of the things you want to do or be. Now, start a second list of what gets in the way of these. If you look at an item and have no idea what's in your way, do it right now. Seriously - I'll still be here when you come back.

Did you go and do it? If not, why didn't you? Write THAT down too.

From this starting point, you can also assess three key areas to help you create your list. These are areas I find where my patients in clinical practice often need more barriers so they can create the life they desire.

Relationships

Are there any relationships in your life where they are not moving you forward in some of these goals? This evaluation is not about calling people out, making things awkward, or forcing you into big life decisions. Let's just start acknowledging where these things are. You can also have a relationship that gives you overall satisfaction but is still holding you back in one area.

Many of my patients have a family relationship that goes in that category.

Relationships With Children

Maybe you have young kids at home. You want to spend time with them, and they need supervision. Because of this, perhaps you don't have time to do something you did before you had children - like going to the gym or making it out to the golf course every weekend.

Acknowledging this is helpful. You are not blaming your children, but you are acknowledging that some of your commitments are barriers to achieving your goals.

Relationships With A Partner

The same may be true of your spouse. Maybe your wife is a night owl and would rather stay up later than you. Maybe your husband never eats breakfast. If you want to do something differently from your spouse, you need to be honest and get on the same page about it. You don't have to do things together, but it can be a problem if you have different expectations.

Let's say you want to start waking up earlier so that you have time to go for a run or eat breakfast. If your partner is saying "your alarm is annoying" or "it's too early! Stay in bed with me," it's going to be harder to set your alarm and get up to make breakfast than if they say "awesome idea! I'm so proud of you."

Again, it isn't your partner's fault if they hate your alarm being early. Frankly - if your alarm disrupts their sleep and they don't want it going off at that hour, that is important. This entire process is a balancing act of the things you want and some of the compromises you are currently making. This is why getting clarity is so important.

Example: Someone Else's Children

Let's say that you are always watching someone else's children. Maybe those are your nieces and nephews. Perhaps there are grandkids; maybe you're trying to help your sister out. I don't know. You might feel like it's tough for you to get to the gym or sign up for a class because you're always watching these kids, or you need to be available to watch them. Then that's a relationship that needs a boundary for you to be able to do what it is you decided you want to say yes to; what it is that you want more of in your life.

Remember You Cannot Read Minds

I know these things can sound scary. You might think, "Well, they're going to be mad at me," or "They're not going to like me." You might think, "It's going to change our relationship." Remember, whenever you're thinking that you know what someone else is thinking - you don't actually have that superpower. You could be wrong. Things could play out differently.

As someone with anxiety, I know you've got many superpowers. You are incredibly creative. You are fantastic at manifesting things. One thing that I have yet to see is someone who can reliably know what someone else is thinking, without asking them. When you catch yourself saying, "Well, if I do this, then that will happen." I want you to stop and create at least one different possibility.

If you're thinking, "well, if I ask my husband to cook or ask my wife to watch the kids instead of me watching them…" Or, "if I tell my brother or my sister that I can't watch their kids…" If I do any of those things, then they're not going to like me. Well, try a different story. Maybe if you do that, then they ask someone else. What if that's the real end of that story?

For any boundaries where insurmountable barriers come up, just try and tell yourself a different story as you make that list. Again, you don't have to do anything right now. You're not calling someone and saying, "Oh, you know how I often watch your kids - I'm not doing it anymore."

You're just saying, "Hey, there is a part of this relationship that 'is not supporting what I've just realized I need; what I want to say 'yes' to; what I want to be doing more of. This relationship is something in the way of that thing right now." That's all we're identifying. Relationships are the first thing.

Technology
The next area you can consider is technology. If you're not getting enough sleep, but your phone is always beside you at bedtime, maybe that's not the right place for your phone to live. How much time are you spending on social media or your cell phone each day? How much time looking at emails? Is it spread throughout your day, interrupting your flow and concentration? Or does it happen in defined blocks? How is your use of technology getting in the way of you getting what you want?

Substances
Are you using any substances or food in a way that is not helping you achieve your highest potential? Sometimes the answer to this is obvious. I have asked this question to hundreds of people, and often people know right away, or quite quickly, what they wish they used differently. Wine. Cigarettes. Beer. Diet Coke. Cannabis. Dessert. Cocaine. Candy. Porn. Scotch. Coffee. Pick your poison; everyone has something where they think, "maybe I'm relying on this too much."

At this point, it is worth noting that this is not an addictions book, and I am not an addictions counsellor. It is possible that, during this exploration, you may think, "maybe I have an addiction to *insert your vice here*." If so, I highly recommend you also seek professional insight and possibly counselling from an expert in this area.

Getting to the bottom of it
Now your list is started, but usually, you can take it much further. Take each item point and ask yourself "why" This will guide you to a deeper understanding of what's truly in your way. The goal of this is to understand both the practical barriers and the subconscious beliefs - or the things you tell yourself about why you can't do something. This more in-depth examination is so we can address both your subconscious beliefs and the practical barriers currently holding you back. This is so you can create a life in

alignment with your values. This is so you can develop habits that create calm from the inside out.

Let's take the example of getting up early to run and flesh out the barriers.

Why don't I do that?

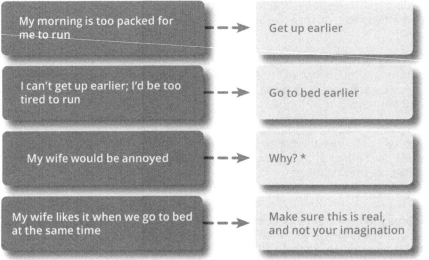

My morning is too packed for me to run	Get up earlier
I can't get up earlier; I'd be too tired to run	Go to bed earlier
My wife would be annoyed	Why? *
My wife likes it when we go to bed at the same time	Make sure this is real, and not your imagination

*remember you are not a mind reader

Possible Practical Solutions

Go to bed earlier alone

Talk to your wife in case she wans to go to bed earlier, too.

Find a different time to go for your run and block that time.

Get to the Bottom of WHY you aren't doing it

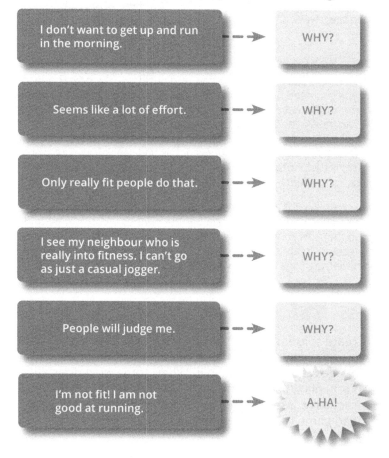

I don't want to get up and run in the morning. → WHY?

Seems like a lot of effort. → WHY?

Only really fit people do that. → WHY?

I see my neighbour who is really into fitness. I can't go as just a casual jogger. → WHY?

People will judge me. → WHY?

I'm not fit! I am not good at running. → A-HA!

The Power of "I Am"

When you reach the "I am" statement, you've hit gold. This statement is where you find your beliefs about yourself, which are the things holding you back from changing the behaviour.

The Solution to this is to write a more balanced "I am" statement. In this example we might say "I haven't practiced running, so I'm not good at it yet. With practice, I will be good at running."

Creating a Concious Life

This is the core of what boundaries are about. They are about making sure that you've got a life you've consciously said 'yes' to. They are about making sure that you are enthusiastic about your life and that you're able to say 'yes' to things that light you up and 'no' to things that don't.

What I love about this approach to boundaries is that it's empowering. It puts it back on you so that you can say, "Look, I want to have a family dinner, but the way my commute is, the way my work is, you know, by the time I cook dinner, we're tired, and it's late." This approach then says, "yes - all these things are true. So, what are you going to do about it?"

Setting Your Boundaries

This is the point where you get to be creative and decide what kind of boundaries you need. Maybe you need boundaries around kids' activities. Maybe there need to be nights where no kids have activities so that you can create boundaries to protect some family dinners. Maybe you need to establish some boundaries in terms of your commute, and see if you can commute at different times. Or - I'm getting crazy here - think about moving so that your commute is not as bad. Don't freak out. Those are just ideas, right? This is the brainstorming part. 'You don't need to feel like you have to do any of these things. You should feel like it's okay to consider all of the possibilities.

But really, what can you do? Is technology interfering with your family dinner as well? Maybe you need a basket where you collect all the phones before dinner and then go plug them in so that everybody can be present. In a scenario like this, you may need something you could create some ritual around, some routine, to set yourself up so that you can have the things that you want. Something that is going to support your boundaries.

Take Action ✏️

Create solutions for what is holding you back from what you want as you read this book and implement the changes recommended in it. When something doesn't go as you plan, use this model to sort out what is in the way practically. Use this chapter and the next to sort out the head game for making these kinds of changes.

Chapter Three
DECISION MINDSET

DO YOU REALLY WANT IT? CAN YOU THINK OF A TIME WHEN YOU WANTED something so bad that you were willing to take a big risk? Risk looking silly. Risk your friends and family not taking you seriously? Risk time. Risk losing money. Risk your reputation.

On February the 14th of 2008, I was at The Albion Hotel. This is a bar known first for being haunted by the ghost of Al Capone's mistress, and second for its Thursday night "Funk Nights," where you could find all of my theatre friends. This particular Thursday night, I was there for a friend's birthday / anti-Valentines Day party. I'm sure when I agreed to attend, I was not expecting to meet the love of my life.

But there he was: tall, handsome, sticking out like a sore thumb in his Aggie[2] jacket. An introverted country-boy / science nerd away from his herd of classmates in a room full of spot-light lovers. Did I know his last name? No. But he caught me without trying. Hook, Line and Sinker.

Of course, convincing him of this took a little more effort. I was 19 and had never pursued anyone before, so I had to become someone I'd never been before. Braver. Bolder.

I wanted to dance, so I asked him to join me on the dance floor.

I wanted to sit beside him, so I did.

I wanted him to call me, so I gave him my number, unsolicited, you know, "in case you need this."

It sounds now like I'm just this person who does these things.

The truth is I'd never done something like that before, and I never have since. That's because I ended up marrying him. I didn't need experience to be bold and ask for what I wanted. At that moment, I chose to become a person who could do that.

That girl who rather than looking at the guy all night and then saying, "Wow, I wish he'd asked for my number," threw caution to the wind and just gave it to him. That choice quite literally changed my life.

Your Turn To Decide

So, my question is for you is: Do you want this? Do you want more calm? Less anxiety? More authenticity? More peace of mind? Less overthinking? More acting? The system I teach in this book has worked for many people.

It's worked for men in sales who had anxiety before their sales calls and meetings. They are able to overcome that anxiety and be confident in their sales meetings.

It's worked for moms overwhelmed with taking care of their kids and trying to find a place for themselves.

It's worked for men in academia who had to travel and do presentations.

It's worked for women with big jobs in finance with job pressures and family obligations, who feel the weight of the world on their shoulders.

It's worked for men in upper management who had a lot of people depending on their team; men who needed to be at their best for their team, to stand up for their team's best interests, and then also to hold down their personal lives and be pillars there as well.

This system has even worked for folks who were unemployed, where their anxiety had prevented them from working to their full potential. This system has now helped them find jobs.

The reason this has worked for so many different people is that they all WANTED it. They wanted something different, and they wanted it badly enough that they were all willing to take a risk by stepping outside of their comfort zone.

Anxiety is overexpression of fear. The fear manifests in judgments; you know the things you say to yourself that bring you down and get in your way and the things that other people have said to you - that you repeat in your head, letting past words of other people dictate your future.

It's time to say no to that crap and do something that scares you.

Stepping Back into the Drivers Seat

Take a minute right now, and commit to yourself, commit to this process, commit to doing something to fortify your mind, body, and spirit.

Seriously, say this to yourself: "I am not going to be ruled by my anxiety." Write it down: "I am not going to make decisions from a place of fear." Shout it out: "I am calm." There is always going to be a reason to be afraid; Do it anyway.

I want you to imagine for a moment what your life would be like if your important life decisions were made by you and not your anxiety.

How would that change your job or your career?

How would that change your personal life, your kids, your relationship with your partner, your friend and peer relationships, your family? What would it look like if it was you driving those situations, and not anxiety?

How about your time off? How would this affect your evenings? Your weekends? Your vacations? Are there places that you would like to go that you haven't because of anxiety? Are there people that you want to spend more time with, but you've been holding yourself back?

You are the one that can decide to take over the steering wheel of your life. You can decide to jump back in the driver's seat.

Let's do this.

Take Action ✎

Write a list of everything that would be different if you weren't feeling anxious.

Chapter Four

TAKING INVENTORY

WHEN YOU PLAN A ROAD TRIP, YOU NEED TWO THINGS. YOU USUALLY HAVE AN idea of where you want to end up – a concert, a theme park or the cottage you rented. But equally important is to know your current location. This information lets you plan how you are going to get where you are going and what stops you want to make along the way.

Identifying Your Starting Point

Before we hit the ground running with managing your life, so it has the calm and peace you desire, we must take a minute to figure out where you are right now. We can do this by stopping and taking inventory. Being honest about your starting place is as important as knowing where you want to go. It's your map, and if you don't know where you are on the map, you can't plan your journey. So we are going to find your starting place.

This inventory is going to guide you through the 5 Pillars of Performance. Each of these pillars is tied not just to your anxiety levels but your overall health and wellness. Most importantly, this inventory connects to how well you can perform, whether that's life, parenthood or business. By being honest with each of these pillars, you can really know where to focus your effort, and what to let slide.

Pillar #1 - Nutrition

Imagine for a minute that you have a car, and not just any car, a high-performance car. You have a Ferrari. What are you filling your tank with? High performance fuel? Or cheap and dirty stuff? Is your engine running on empty? Or do you make sure there is never less than a 1/4 of a tank?

Here's the thing: you ARE the car. Your body is the Ferrari, and your food is the fuel. How are you treating it? Are you feeding it high-performance fuel? Are you heading out on a long trip before filling her up? Or are you taking proper care of him so he can perform at the highest level?

Take Action 🖉

For the next week, take a written inventory of everything you put in your body. Track the veggies and the water. The coffee and the pastry. The fruit and the bread and chips and the beer. Do this not to judge yourself, but to understand what you are eating.

Pillar #2 - Sleep

How many hours of sleep are you getting each night?

How much time do you leave in your day for sleep?

When do you go to bed and how long do you spend there before you fall asleep? What do you do in that time? Are you turning the light off, or playing games on your phone. Are you watching tv until you can't keep your eyes open anymore or brushing your teeth and falling asleep as soon as your head hits the pillow?

Do you sleep through the night? Do you wake up or toss and turn all night?

Getting real about the quality and quantity of your sleep is vital.

Sleep is the reset button for your brain. It's how the supercomputer between your ears de-fragments. It's where you discharge your emotions from today, so you can wake up ready to respond instead of yelling at everyone or bursting into tears. It increases your bandwidth, lowers your blood pressure and helps your memory.

Figure out where your sleep is at. Honestly. Then we can make it better.

Take Action 🖉

Describe your sleep habits. How much sleep do you get, and what is your current before-bed routine?

Pillar #3 - Exercise

Next is the activity inventory. This is a place to just catch up with yourself and think about things like, "Oh, how much am I actually exercising right now?" Write down what you did last week, even if it wasn't a typical week. We regularly have weeks that aren't typical, and we delude ourselves as to our starting point by saying, "I work out three times a week," when it's really two. Don't start with what you should do; start with what you do now.

Then, think about a time in your life where you were successful with your exercise. Write down what you were doing then if it's different from what last week was (as it often is).

We will use both of these pieces in a later chapter to build out your full exercise plan and the path to get you from where you are to where you are going to be.

Take Action 🖉

Write out your exercise habits, as they are and as you wish them to be.

Pillar #4 - Mindfulness

Life is full of interruptions. Cell phones. Emails. Kids. There is always somewhere else for your attention to be. It's hard to focus.

That's where mindfulness comes in. The idea of mindfulness is that you bring a level of non-judgmental awareness to the present moment.

Maybe you've heard of mindfulness before; it might even be something you already have a daily practice around. If that's you - great! Maybe mindfulness is new to you - that's Ok too.

The point right now is to find out, "Is there any mindfulness meditation in your life?" If you are a daily (or like me, an occasional meditator) - you know the answer to this. But even if the concept of mindfulness is new to you, it doesn't mean that you are starting at zero. You likely have some kind of mindfulness practice you just we not labelling it that way.

Maybe you have a prayer practice. Include a prayer practice in this as there is a lot of brain research that shows similar brain benefits for prayer and meditation. So while I understand that they are not the same thing and that they mean different things to different people, we want to count it.

Maybe you had a therapist teach you a breathing exercise at some point in time. Maybe you picked a breathing exercise in a yoga class, and you do that whenever you start stressing; let's count that.

Any practice you have that helps you stop and reorient to right now and what's happening in your body. We want to start paying attention to so we can expand this practice.

A lot of the time, when people think about meditation and mindfulness practices, they think of sitting alone in a room. While that is one style of meditation, that is just one way to engage in this.

Any activity can be a mindful activity if you bring your full awareness to it.

For some folks running is a mindfulness activity. Personally, I like yoga. Other people knit, colour or make other art. It doesn't matter what it is - if it brings you into NOW into your body. Count it.

Take Action 🖉

Write down any meditation, prayer or breathwork practices you are currently using and any you have used at other times in your life. Also, note any hobbies you use to make yourself feel calm.

Pillar #5 - Connection

When it comes to anxiety, different lifestyle factors affect how you're feeling. We are going to use the concept of connection to address many of these factors. There are three parts to connection: connection to yourself, connection to others, and the connection to something bigger.

When it comes to anxiety, different lifestyle factors affect how you're feeling. We are going to use the concept of connection to address many of these factors. There are three parts to connection: connection to yourself, connection to others, and the connection to something bigger.

So in the first part, the connection to self, that's really about what's your identity. Self Esteem, Self Belief and Identity and Purpose all come under this 'connection to self' pillar. For some people, this is an easy pillar. They know who they are. They don't have any anxiety around it. But for other people, this can be the crux or a significant contributing factor to anxiety[3].

The second part covers social support. What's your social circle like? Loneliness has a considerable impact on mental health, and we know that mental and physical health measures are better when people are socially connected[4]. This is not about judging yourself. This is about being realistic and understanding what resources you have to move forward with, and so if you have a strong social support network, you should put it in. If you feel like your support system is okay, but it could be better, be honest about that. If you've been socially isolating and are worried about your social support network, take note. I want you to consider what it would take to be able to expand your social connections, and how that would improve your health, and how that, in turn, would improve your life.

Then, the last part is a connection to something bigger. Whatever your beliefs are about life here on this planet - this is a question for you. I don't care if you are Christian, Muslim, Jewish, Buhddist, Atheist, or you are undecided. For this exercise, we aren't judging WHAT you think about this world. Again, we are just taking stock. What in this world do you think about beyond your immediate life and family? Do you believe in God? Do you let things go to the universe? Do you ask your ancestors for signs and guidance? Maybe you love looking for little connections in mathematics! It doesn't matter how much or little attention you pay to this. Just get clear on what you believe.

The last thing I want you to do for this part is just to take a minute to think about the last time you felt wonder. When was the last time you encountered something that made you feel awe? Was it a painting? A bird? A piece of music? A sunset? Write a little bit about that and where you can encounter that in life, and we'll start from there.

---

[3]Steffens, N. K., LaRue, C. J., Haslam, C., Walter, Z. C., Cruwys, T., Munt, K. A., Haslam, S. A., Jetten, J., & Tarrant, M. (2019). Social identification-building interventions to improve health: a systematic review and meta-analysis. Health psychology review, 1–28. Advance online publication. https://doi.org/10.1080/17437199.2019.1669481https://doi.org/10.1080/17437199.2019.1669481

[4] Rico-Uribe, L. A., Caballero, F. F., Martín-María, N., Cabello, M., Ayuso-Mateos, J. L., & Miret, M. (2018). Association of loneliness with all-cause mortality: A meta-analysis. PloS one, 13(1), e0190033. https://doi.org/10.1371/journal.pone.0190033

Take Action

Journal your thoughts on the following questions: What in your life helps you feel connected to yourself? What helps you connect with others in an aunthenic way? Where to you find beauty and meaning in the world?

Tranquil Toolkit

As you take note of your starting line, you should take a minute to look at the tools you already have. This chapter is all about inventorying and categorizing your tools for anxiety, and I call this your tranquil toolkit. We will start with an inventory of what you do and what you take to overcome your anxiety, on an ongoing basis or "in the moment".

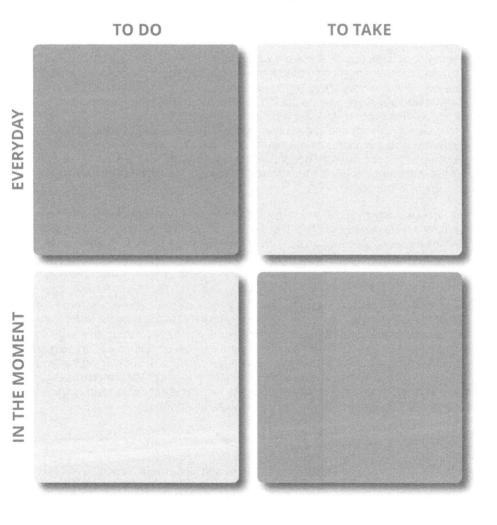

This is a place where you can fill in your own resources. It's blank for a reason because everybody has their own tools. I'm going to talk about what types of things you might want to put in, and you can grab yours and fill in what's true to you. You may also want to consider making some notes about things that you might want to include or reflect on.

Tools to prevent feeling anxious

The top two boxes are things you do every day, so these are things that are part of your daily routine. You do them in the morning or you do them in the evening, and you always make sure to do them and you know that they support your mental health. For example someone who has a daily prayer or meditation practice or who goes to the gym every day might put that in this list. I would say for now, if it's four times a week, put it in, this is something that you are doing, it's a behaviour. The other thing that you might have is something that you're taking every day. This could be a medication, this could be a supplement, anything that you are taking every day that supports your mental wellness, you can put it in this category.

Tools for when you are feeling anxious

The bottom two boxes are for support you use "in the moment." This is what you're doing when you become overwhelmed; when you have an anxiety attack, an anxiety moment, or a panic attack. These are your resources. Again, they are divided. In the "Things to do" there might be a breathing exercise that you know of, (and if you don't have any don't worry we are going to cover some in the next chapter) But if you've got one that works well, you want to put it down. The next thing that you should consider is adding any training or techniques you have learned in your life up until this point. Maybe you've been in therapy and know some cognitive-behavioural techniques. Maybe there is something your grandma always said that you repeat to yourself when you are always overwhelmed. If you have any mindfulness techniques that you use "in the moment," you can put that there. If there is a friend that you call or anything else you think of that you do, you put in this box.

The last box is anything that you take at the moment that you are dealing with anxiety. If you have a relief remedy, whether that's a natural, whether that's a pharmaceutical, this is where it goes so that you can see, "oh, these are the things that I can take when I'm feeling anxious."

Checking for a balanced toolkit

It starts dividing your tools, and you get a very visual picture between what you are taking versus the things you are doing. What resources do you have for when you are feeling anxious versus the things to prevent anxiety. The goal, moving forward, is to bring in some more balance to the diagram. We want to avoid a situation where you have a giant list of things that you take when you're feeling anxious, but nothing that you're doing every day to help you not feel anxious in the first place. We want to make sure that you've got things in all of the quadrants to help bring down your overall anxiety consistently, but also to help you manage any ups and downs.

Take Action ✏

Go through your current resources and kit out your tranquil toolkit.

Chapter Five
JUST BREATHE

"JUST BREATHE," I HEARD A VOICE STATING THROUGH MY OWN LOUD AND FAST breaths. At that moment, I wanted to punch them in the face.

Couldn't they hear me breathing?!? I'm trying over here! Gasping for each inhale in shaky pieces only to have it rush out of my body and leave me clamouring for more air.

I had just walked out of a restaurant where I was gathered with friends to celebrate a friend's birthday. My thoughts were spinning so fast it was making me dizzy, or perhaps it was the lack of oxygen getting to my brain because, at that moment, it certainly wasn't getting enough.

I didn't know this then, but between arguing with my husband that he couldn't come to the party, showing up to the party without my husband, realizing this was a thing I could have brought my spouse too, and feeling bad about it all, I was primed for a panic attack.

Add on the social pressure to do a celebratory shot (not my style) and the alcohol of said shot (fuel for the anxious fire). It was no wonder I started having a panic attack.

Hearing "Just Breathe" is the most frustrating thing to hear at that moment.

And people say it all the time, because - and this is the annoying part - it works.

I know, anxiety makes it difficult to breathe. It's one of the symptoms. And if it were that easy as "just breathing," then we all wouldn't be having this conversation right now. So I am not going to tell you "just to breathe," but I do want to empower you with the knowledge of what breathing does to your nervous system, and I want to talk to you about how practicing breathing in advance makes it more accessible "in the moment."

Then I want to give you three specific breathing exercises that I use in my practice that have helped my patients overcome their anxiety. The reason I give three is that not every breathing exercise works for every person, and so certain ones are going to work better for you. Your job is to try them out and see which ones work for you.

What breathing does for your body
Your autonomic nervous system controls your body. It's different than the nervous system you use to type and throw a ball. It runs automatically and takes care of things like your digestion, your heartbeat and your pupil size; you know, systems you have

better things to do than continuously regulate. It has two modes; sympathetic and parasympathetic, which can't both be on at the same time. The sympathetic is the stressed state. When you're having an anxiety attack, you are in a stressed state. Your heart rate goes up, maybe your breathing increases, you might feel tense, you might get some digestive symptoms. All of that is because of this sympathetic nervous system activation. What we want to do is move the nervous system back into the parasympathetic state - to a calm state. The coolest thing is that you have the power to do that. You can change your nervous system by controlling your breath.

Just take a minute to have that sink in for a minute. This automatic nervous system is running on autopilot over here, causing you to freak out, and you can intervene. You have that much power over your physiology[5]. This blows my mind. If it's not blowing your mind, then that's fine, but this blows my mind. The more I think about it, the cooler it is.

Once you realize how powerful that is, you are probably going to start wondering how to do that.

The first thing to know is when you're in a stressful situation, its difficult to learn and bring in new behaviours, which is why all of these exercises, these breathing exercises, it's important to practice them when you're calm. I recommend that you find time in the morning - honestly all you need is two minutes - and again at night. Seriously just two minutes to practise these breathing exercises. When you practise these things when you're calm, you build the neural pathways - your brain's memory of what to do - so that when you're feeling anxious, you don't have to think about it. Your neural pathways are already ready to go, and your brain knows what to do.

Practicing in advance allows you to have access to these tools when you need them.

Let's get into them.

4-Square Breathing

The first one we are going to try is four-square breathing, also called box breathing. First, inhale for a count of four, then hold that inhale for four. Next, exhale for the count of four. Finally, hold that exhale for four.

Take a minute to try a couple of them right now. Breathe in two, three, four, hold two, three, four, Out two, three, four, hold two, three, four. Do it at least four times, or until you feel your body relax.

While you are doing it, you can draw a box, or if you're in a meeting, you can just imagine the box in your mind's eye. That works very well as well.

Combining breathing with the imagination of the box works in two ways. The first is controlling the breath through the vagus nerve and activating the parasympathetic nervous system, moving the body from a stress response to a relaxed response. The other thing that happens with box breathing is that it occupies your mind.

When you are counting and focusing your mind on imagining a box, and your thinking

[5] Hopper, S. I., Murray, S. L., Ferrara, L. R., & Singleton, J. K. (2019). Effectiveness of diaphragmatic breathing for reducing physiological and psychological stress in adults: a quantitative systematic review. JBI database of systematic reviews and implementation reports, 17(9), 1855–1876. https://doi.org/10.11124/JBISRIR-2017-003848

gets focused on that, it works as a bit of a distraction from whatever you were thinking or worrying about. In this way, it acts as a mindfulness activity and pulls you into the present moment.

Air Arc

I hope you enjoyed the four square breathing exercise. If you didn't, do not worry; there are many others from which to choose. I call this the air arc breathing, and it comes from my singing background. Singing, incidentally, has also been shown to decrease anxiety[6]. I suspect that a lot of that has to do with breathing.

For this one, you are going to need your hands. Put one hand on your belly button and the other one in front of your face, extending your arm all the way out. Next, take a deep breath in, fill up your entire belly. Feel your abdomen with the hand on your belly. Focus on the sensation in your belly and on your hand as you feel your belly button rise.

Then, in a clear and controlled way, you are going to exhale. Blow like you are softly blowing across the flame of the candle, you want to make it flicker - but not blow out! You're going to be able to feel the air on your hand, and you want to notice that sensation.

Now, if you don't want to put your hand out, what you can do is practice with an actual candle. You can even imagine that there's a candle, that the airflow is going over the top of that candle, and that the flame is just flickering, not burning out.

What you are working on in this exercise is a consistent, long exhale. Practice really filling up your whole lungs, and as long, controlled of an exhale as you can make. You want to do this for about two minutes.

Alternate Nostril Breathing

The last of the three breathing exercises I'm teaching is a form of yogic breathing called alternate nostril breathing, and so if you that have a yoga practice, you may have seen this one before. Whether or not you've seen it, it doesn't matter - this is excellent breathing practice.

The way this one works is that you breathe in through one nostril and then you breathe out through the other, and then you bring the air in this way, and out the other one.

First, you need to bend the middle three fingers of your left hand in so they touch your palm, leaving out your thumb and your pinky finger. You will use your fingers to block each of your nostrils in turn, alternating which nostril you breathe from (hence the alternate nostril breathing)

Try it now by blocking the right nostril with the pinky finger of your left hand and breathing in. Now switch, let your pinky finger away from the left nostril and use your thumb to cover the right nostril. So now you're blocking the nostril that you just inhaled through, and then you exhale through the other one. At the end of that exhalation, when you've let all your air out, take a breath through the right side, continuing to hold

---

[6] Daykin, N., Mansfield, L., Meads, C., Julier, G., Tomlinson, A., Payne, A., Grigsby Duffy, L., Lane, J., D'Innocenzo, G., Burnett, A., Kay, T., Dolan, P., Testoni, S., & Victor, C. (2018). What works for wellbeing? A systematic review of wellbeing outcomes for music and singing in adults. Perspectives in public health, 138(1), 39–46. https://doi.org/10.1177/1757913917740391

your thumb to your left nostril. Then switch back, so you exhale on the left side. Keep switching back after each inhalation.

Again, do this for two to five minutes every day. This is not one of the exercises that I find particularly helpful "in the moment" for most people. When you're feeling anxious, it's a little tricky to block off your airways intentionally. That can be a little bit more anxiety-provoking. I more recommended this one if you enjoy it as part of daily practice, whereas some of the other ones, the box breathing and the air arc, work a little bit better "in the moment."

Take Action

Set aside some time each day to breathe. Put it in you calendar or set a phone alarm.

NUTRITION

Chapter Six

IMPORTANCE OF EATING ENOUGH

YOU AREN'T YOUR BEST WHEN YOU'RE HUNGRY.

When I was in university, my girlfriends had this term for me, "Hurricane Katie" As you can imagine, hurricane Katie came in like a storm. She was furious. She might cry, or she might yell - you couldn't tell in advance.

One time, my friends and I were at the grocery store when one of my friends grabbed some toilet paper. A normal enough choice, however, this toilet paper was not made of 100% recycled paper.

Enter Hurricane Katie.

"Are you seriously going to wipe your ass with the boreal forest," I yelled. It may have been a good point, but this was surely not the best way to make it.

Initially, 'Hurricane Katie' seemed to show up out of the blue. But as I paid more attention I got the bottom of it; I was hungry. I'm not my best self when I'm hungry. You aren't either. Don't take offence - none of us are[7]!

There's a study that looked at restricting calories to create "semi-starvation"[8]. The group were healthy, mind and body when they started the study, but they really didn't cope well with not having enough food. They got depressed, they started cheating on the study and stealing food some of them had to be let out of the study for suicidal ideation! They weren't able to follow through with decisions that they'd made before they started this restricted caloric diet.

'Dieting' is semi starvation

All of this was on a 1600-kilocalorie diet. Maybe you've never counted calories, and you don't have a concept of how little food that is. I'm happy for you.

If you've ever tried dieting, you realize that in a lot of our current conversations around diet, 1600 kilocalories is often treated as a fairly normal daily intake of calories. This is not "fairly normal".

During naturopathic medical school, I was taught to prescribe a daily diet of 1500 kilocalories for things like weight-loss, cardiovascular health, and diabetes. Problematically for mental health, 1600 kilocalories will feel much like the conditions of "semi-starvation," which I described earlier.

This is not good.

Now causal links between hunger and anxiety/depression are not uniformly backed by medical literature. However, this book is based on my own clinical experience. In that experience, I have seen far more benefit when an anxious or depressed client are supported in eating enough calories than when they go on diet with severe caloric restrictions.

Of course there are other considerations to make here, and you should not make any drastic changes to your diet or exercise regime without consulting with your medical professional, especially if you have any pre-existing conditions.

Your brain runs on food

That being said, the first thing I want to highlight is that your brain needs calories to function. Your brain runs on calories. It uses calories as fuel. It also uses calories to communicate with itself, and with the rest of your body. Aside from the simplicity of calories (energy), your brain needs different types of macronutrients.

The first thing your brain needs is carbohydrates. That's the type of food that you get from bread, pasta, grains, and fruit. Carbohydrates break down into glucose (sugar). This is the main fuel for your brain; your brain likes to run on sugar. If your body doesn't have enough sugar from eating carbohydrates, your liver will go to extensive effort to make sure that there's enough sugar in your body so that your brain can function.

The next macronutrient that your brain likes is protein. Your brain communicates with molecules called neurotransmitters. Your nervous system makes these from amino acids, which come in your diet from protein. Your brain talks to your body through neurotransmitters. When you think of it this way - you want to make sure that protein is abundant for your brain to make all the neurotransmitters it needs to talk to your body.

The last macronutrient that we're going to talk about for your brain is fat. Your brain is largely made of fat. Fat is the insulation around the wires that makes your brain work. Your brain needs a lot of quality fats to be the best brain it can be.

So, in summary: fats are the substance of your brain, carbs are the fuel for your brain, and protein is how your brain communicates. You need all of these pieces.

This leads me back to: You need to eat enough food.

The next question I know you are thinking is: "how much is enough?"

How much food is 'enough'

The problem with answering that in a book is that everybody (and every body) is different. You are different in terms of your muscle mass, your body composition, how tall you are, and how you exercise. Things like your daily activities, even things like the temperature of the room you are in, have some (albeit small) impacts on how much food you need.

So how do you know if you are getting enough food to avoid the negative mood consequences of under-eating? Well, if you are restricting your food intake, you are probably not getting enough. You might be under-eating if you are always cold, or if you're always hungry. Now I don't mean "if you periodically get hungry," - we all get hungry. But if you don't eat when you're hungry, or when you get hungry you eat, and you still feel hungry because you didn't eat enough to satisfy that hunger - you might not be getting enough food. Without enough food, you're not going to have your best mental health.

This is not about weight

Now, as an aside - because I know so many of you are thinking this - this is not about weight. We cannot focus on weight in this book, because frankly, it would be unproductive. If you think that something is going on with your weight, that it is out of balance and you are losing or gaining lots of weight, and you don't know why I do recommend that you see a naturopathic doctor or a functional medical doctor and get an assessment done. It could a serious health concern. It could be a side effect of the medication you're taking. There could be something going on with your hormones that have thrown this out of balance. I cannot possibly answer those questions in this book, but if these are concerns, then it is important that you get those answers.

For mental health, we're not going to focus on weight loss, because it is detrimental. If you're up for it, I recommend that you throw out your scale. You don't need it. It's not helping your physical health, and it's definitely not helping your mental health.

Instead, we're going to focus the nutrition portion of this book on optimizing the building blocks your brain and body needs for health. Everything we talked about is about increasing your confidence when it comes to making food choices and understanding nutrition and health.

Chapter Seven
EATING REGULARLY

REMEMBER BACK TO TAKING INVENTORY WHEN YOU DID THE DIET DIARY?
Now's a good time to pull it up and look at it. The first question you are going to ask
is "Am I eating regularly?" By that, I mean things like: are you eating breakfast? are you
eating every four to six hours when you are awake? These are really important for your
mental health. I know they sound super obvious, but it is so important that you keep
your blood sugar even throughout the day. The best way to do that is to get up, get
some fuel into you. We'll talk next about what that fuel is. For now, let's just make sure
you're getting fuel in, and that you are planning so that you can eat every four to six
hours from that point on.

Step 1: Break your fast
I'll give you an example. I typically wake up at 6:30, so I want to be eating my breakfast
by 7:00. That's ideal for me. Now I get it! You have a job and kids, and you are trying to
find time to work out and meditate and the hundreds of other things to do you have to
do in a day!

But really look at trying to find some time to get something into your body within that
first 30 minutes of your day. If you're not eating breakfast at all right now, just get
something - anything - into you that you would consider breakfast in your life. That's the
entire task for you.

If you are already eating breakfast, I want you to look at what it is. Is it really within that
first 30 minutes of waking up? If it's not, can we put it there? Can we get you some fuel
to start your day? Maybe it's a shake. Perhaps you're used to eating eggs, and you're
not sure that you can get them in that quickly. Well, maybe that looks like you - in your
kitchen - eating an apple while you are making eggs because making the eggs, on top of
everything else you are wrangling in your house in the morning, takes longer than those
minutes.

That is really what the goal is, is to get you eating breakfast.

Step 2: Watch your intervals
Then the second part of eating regularly is looking at the frequency of your meals and
snacks and seeing if you get some food into your body every four to six hours. Why do
we want to do this? Because it helps you manage your blood sugar.

I want to suggest to you that if you're going more than six hours without eating and you find yourself feeling anxious that - at that moment - the feeling might not be anxiety. It is possible that your blood sugar has crashed, and it is just your body telling you that it's hungry.

Those two sensations feel a lot alike!

You get kind of shaky, lightheaded; something feels off. Our brains are storytelling machines. If your mind is used to feeling anxious and tells a story that goes, "I am anxious," or, "I have anxiety," then when your body starts feeling off and it gets so shakiness, then your brain fills in the blanks saying, "Oh, I'm anxious." This is one of the ways the conditions of our bodies can affect the stories that we tell in our minds.

So we want to make sure that this isn't happening for you!

Make sure that you're eating three to four times a day! Don't go for more than six hours without eating. No, we aren't including overnight right now. You can easily spend 12 hours not eating overnight so long as you aren't getting hungry. You can not eat from 7:00 to 7:00 and be totally fine. However, make sure that while you're awake, you're nourishing yourself.

Step 3: Make a plan
Grab a calendar and schedule your meals out. Look at this week or pick a typical week. I recommend that you do this week, even if its "not typical." I find that the more we exclude our life looking for what's "usual," the less we understand what "usual" actually is for ourselves. Take some time to figure out when you're going to eat. Consider things like when you're going to work and any obligations that keep you from eating when you want to. Plan when you are going to have breakfast.

Step 4: Mind the gaps
Make sure to check the timing between your meals; if you're eating breakfast at 6:00 AM and then your lunch break at work isn't until 1:00, that's probably too long. You might want to figure out how to get like a snack in there somewhere.

The other area to watch is the time between lunch and dinner. I often see that my patients eat their lunch at 11:30 or 12:00 at work. By the time they get their kids, get home, cook something and sit down to eat, it is seven o'clock at night or later. So if you're eating dinner at 7:00 and you're having lunch at noon, you need a snack. You need to put something in that mid-afternoon slot. Otherwise, you're going to walk in the door, and you're ravenous. That really takes away from being able to eat a proper meal. This can also make you really anxious while getting home, not being your best self while you're trying to transition from work into home life.

Do some work now, and make sure that you are setting yourself up. Putting a break or a planned snack in there is going to make a lot of difference.

Take Action 🖊

Grab a calendar and schedule your meals out.

Chapter Eight

PROTEIN AND PRODUCE

AFTER YOU'VE SORTED OUT WHEN YOU'RE SUPPOSED TO EAT, YOU MAY HAVE thought, okay, but what am I going to eat? This chapter is going to cover the most important answer to the question of what to eat. The answer I want you to think of is the 2 P's: protein and produce.

What counts as protein

While proteins are in all our foods, think of a protein as a food that's got more protein than it has fats or carbohydrates. All food has (some) protein, fat and carbohydrate and we need all of these things. This is important for blood sugar stability and also for making sure we have an abundance of amino acids to build neurotransmitters.

A portion of food is higher in protein when it is mostly built of amino acids. Meat is a classic example, but protein food can be a plant or animal source.

chicken	tuna	chickpeas
beef	shrimp	lentils
pork	eggs	nuts
lamb	yogurt	whey powder
salmon	soybeans	

This list is a starting point, so you can begin to think about what things you like to eat, which are good sources of protein. When you plan or prepare a meal or snack, start by picking one of these protein-rich foods and then pairing with produce.

What counts as produce

When I say produce, I mean fruits or vegetables. It does not matter whether they are fresh or whether they are frozen. It doesn't matter whether it's a fruit or a vegetable; it's just important that you include produce. Most produce is a good source of carbohydrate in your diet. You need this for energy, but it has a lot of other mood-balancing things happening with it.

Fruits and vegetables are the best source of vitamins and minerals. When you eat a wide variety of fruits and vegetables, making sure to have at least one serving of fruits and vegetables every time you eat, it floods nutrients into your body. It also supports your digestive tract and micro-biome with healthy fibre.

Fruit and Vegetable Examples

lettuce	broccoli	pears
cucumber	tomato	mangos
bell peppers	apples	blueberries

Some examples of combinations

You might have something like having an apple with some peanut butter on it as a snack. That's something with a protein as well as produce. Another classic snack is prosciutto-wrapped melon, which is something with fruit and protein together, which makes it a really balancing snack and a good choice. Smoothies are where I see people put fruits, vegetables, and protein powders all in a blender, and then there you go. Depending on how much food you need, a shake is either a great meal or a snack, because it combines all of those essential components in a blender.

When you look at your plate, and you're looking at lunch or dinner, make sure that you've got some protein on there. Is there a little bit of salmon? Is there some egg? How about vegetables? Have you got salad greens going on, or do you have some steamed broccoli?

Don't stop yet

Remember, protein and produce are the starting point - and you can also add more food. Looking at a plate of steamed broccoli and a piece of chicken - that's not going to be enough food for me! So I'm going to need some rice, or I'm going to need a sweet potato with that. You should do that too, adding grains, veggies, and sauces or dressings until it's enough food, and it looks delicious.

Start where you are at

Honestly, the goal is not to become perfect and have a week of perfectly planned meals that you are never going to make. You want to start with where you are and add to it. If you have a take-out breakfast sandwich and you were only grabbing a coffee before, that breakfast is better than nothing! Is it where we want to get you at the end of this program? No, I'll be honest, it isn't. We're going to aim for some really high-quality nutrition, but right now, work on what the next step would be.

Rather than completely change 100% of your meals and snacks, think about what you can add. Maybe there is some protein missing at breakfast, or you can add some produce into your snack. Don't think you have to take all kinds of food out. If you are hungry and you think, "Oh, I want some chocolate covered almonds." Grab some berries and pair them with the chocolate almonds because that's got some protein in it (the nuts) – but there's no produce there. Look at what you're already eating and try to round it out by adding in some protein.

Take Action ✎

Check your meal plan for protein and produce. Add some in where it's missing.

Chapter Nine

BUILDING A BETTER BRAIN
(AND NERVOUS SYSTEM)

YOUR BRAIN IS MADE UP OF NERVES, AND NERVES WORK BY CONDUCTING electrical impulses. Now physics was never my strongest science, and that's fine I'm a naturopathic doctor not a physicist; I do know that to conduct an electrical current down a wire, you need a charge and some insulation.

When it comes to the wiring of your brain - minerals are the charge, and fats are the insulation. To build a better brain, we need to make sure that we have both of these components.

Meet Magnesium

The main mineral for relaxation in your nervous system, and through the muscles in your body is magnesium. We know from nutrition research that many people are not getting enough magnesium, and that's a problem[9]. When there's not enough magnesium, that can wreak havoc on the body by causing anxiety, insomnia, headaches, and muscle tension, among other problems.

You need enough magnesium that you aren't anxious and tense, just from insufficient magnesium! But we don't want to stop at just enough magnesium. We want an abundance of magnesium so that your body is never searching for it.

Where do you get magnesium?

The two common sources of dietary magnesium are leafy green vegetables and in the germ or that outside layer of nuts, grains, and seeds. For a grain to provide a lot of magnesium, they need to be a "whole grain" and still have their germ on. Think brown rice instead of white and whole wheat rather than refined products. Unfortunately, things like white bread and white rice have been refined and processed, which strips away almost all of the magnesium.

Another thing to know about magnesium is that there's less magnesium in our food than there used to be[10]. Magnesium levels in our soil, and therefore, in our food products have been decreasing. One of the things you can do to increase the magnesium in the food that you are eating - besides choosing foods that are higher in magnesium - is choosing organic produce. Organic practices restore magnesium levels in the soil and have higher levels of some nutrients, including 29% more magnesium[11]. So if you have access to organic food, magnesium might be one reason to choose them, particularly for your leafy greens.

When it comes to getting enough magnesium, you may decide that there isn't enough in your diet. If so, remember this is a normal starting place, and you have 80% of people with you on this. Or, you might decide that you can't consistently get enough in your diet. In my clinical practice, this is when we start considering supplementing magnesium - often just for a while as someone works on their diet. If you think you need a magnesium supplement, I recommend that you find a practitioner to work with that can help you with that, such as a naturopathic doctor, nutritionist, or holistic or functional medical doctor.

Fats

Fats are the insulator of the nervous system. They make up the membranes of all the cells of your body. When your cells get injured or damaged, it's the fats that work as signalers of inflammation.

Because of their role as signalers, the types and ratios of fats that make up your cells matter. Some fats make a gentler inflammatory response, making it less dramatic and overall less harmful. To create a more gentle inflammatory response, you need to increase the amount of omega-three fatty acids, compared to the omega-six fatty acids (usually abundant in your diet.)

In particular, when talking about omega-three fatty acids - we want to focus on the long-chain fatty acids DHA and EPA. These fatty acids are important for the brain, are not easily made by the body.

You can get them from your diet, particularly from fatty fish. The acronym for the best fish is called SMASH, which stands for: salmon, mackerel, anchovy, sardines, and herring. Omega-three fatty acids, particularly a fish oil supplement high in EPA, can be taken to support the brain. This has not only been shown to improve depression and anxiety on its own[12], but it increases the efficacy of common medications for these conditions[13]. In this way, omega-three fatty acids are not just supportive of the brain. They are a treatment for mood disorders, all on their own.

As always, you want to consult with your own practitioner to make sure that supplements are safe for you to take, especially if you take medication.

Chapter Ten

WHAT NOT TO EAT

"SO, DO YOU TYPICALLY EAT ANY SNACKS?" I ASK, TRYING TO KEEP MY VOICE casual as I look at the diet diary in front of me.

"No, that's everything I eat," replies the person in the chair across from me.

I grab a sip of water.

I look down again at the list of food, hoping I have missed something. But I know I haven't. I've seen this before.

It's meticulous. It has protein and produce. It has regular intervals. I'm ashamed to think of what a younger version of myself might say to this. "Looks like you eat a very clean diet" or "Wow, good work, you are on top of your nutrition."

I know better now. I know that sometimes this kind of diet diary means my patients are eating too little or monitoring their food too closely to achieve health, a condition called orthorexia.

Sometimes, we get on some kind of health and fitness bandwagon, and we go too far. In our efforts to clean up our diets and make better choices, we go to extremes or make choices for unsustainable reasons.

Searching for health, we end up sick.

This is an advanced manoeuver

I saved this part chapter for the end. I have a love/hate relationship with this stuff because I think it can be vital, and I know how harmful it can be. So I'm going to be upfront: if you have a history of disordered eating, this may not be the chapter for you. It's ok to focus on some other great things, like the nutritional advice we've covered up until now. For some of you, not reading this is the brave choice, and I fully support your decision to skip ahead.

If you've skipped to this chapter, go back, you need to add things to your diet before you start taking things away, and THE MOST BENEFIT comes from adding things.

Now, that being said, some foods are fuel on the fire we call anxiety. These are things that are going to make your anxiety worse rather than help to make it better. And I'd be amiss not to let you know of the things that you can be mindful of, things that you could be reducing that help reduce anxiety.

Sugar

The first thing we're going to talk about is sugar. All the advice in this book up to this point: the eating regularly, the protein, the produce, that's all for the purpose of helping your body maintain well-balanced blood sugar. When you have processed refined sugars, your blood sugar goes up and then it crashes. When your blood sugar crashes like that, it causes jitteriness, lightheadedness and an uncomfortable feeling[14]. Your body is telling you something is off. If you are used to feeling anxious, and you tell yourself, "I have anxiety," then this hypoglycemic feeling that feels a lot like anxiety can trigger your brain telling this story, "I am anxious."

Because of all this, I encourage you to limit the processed sugar you're having. Think about thinks you might eat regularly, like pop or candies – these would be on the top of the list. Next would be things like sweets, baked goods, cookies. How often are those coming into your diet? Then you can consider, where else is there sugar? If you're eating a lot of packaged convenience food, there might be way more sugar than you think! Things like granola bars, cereals, sauces, dressings, condiments, all that kind of thing, all tend to have a lot of sugar in them. Take some time to consider reducing the amount of sugar you are eating according to where you are starting from.

The other thing that sugar does is massively impact your intestinal microbiome. The microbiome is the collection of friendly bacteria that live in your digestive tract and help you along. Everyone has a microbiome, and a healthy one is important for your overall health and wellbeing. I haven't gone into too much detail about how the gut and the brain are connected because it's not necessary to understand the intricacies to be able to make these kinds of changes and improve your anxiety. But it is a way in which your body influences your brain and your mood.

What you eat fuels not just you, but your microbiome. Although your microbiome is mostly made up of friends, there are also enemies who aren't doing you any favours. Those little guys eat up your food and give you nothing but pain and heartbreak (sometimes literally[15]) in return. You don't need to encourage them to hang around. When it comes to food - your friends love fibre, and the enemies - they like sugar. One of the ways to be less hospitable to your enemies is not to feed them very well, so they leave. Reducing the sugar in your diet sends those guys backing out of your microbiome.

Alcohol

Next up - alcohol. What - you didn't think it was helping your anxiety, did you? Alcohol dysregulates your blood sugar, and it depletes your glycogen. Glycogen is the sugar stored in your liver that your liver uses to keep blood sugar nice and even. Alcohol also disrupts your sleep, partly because your liver has trouble maintaining your blood sugar. Plus, alcohol is toxic to your brain, and let's be honest: if it's not good for your brain, and it's not good for anxiety.

I've got a question for you.

Is the way you are interacting with alcohol supporting your health goals?

I'm not going to sit here and tell you what that looks like for you because I don't know. Whether you drink frequently, rarely or never - take a minute to make sure you are honest about your consumption and clear about what you want it to be. Whatever you decide, set a boundary and commit to holding that for yourself. No matter what you do moving forward, be aware that although "in the moment" it might seem like alcohol makes anxiety better[16], it might be making your anxiety worse[17].

Caffeine

Caffeine is fuel on the anxiety fire. It wakes up your adrenal glands and sends out adrenaline. Adrenaline pushes your body into that sympathetic nervous system state we've been working on getting you out of and makes your heart rush, your body jittery, and your bowels move. If you are already a jittery and anxious person, you do not need more caffeine.

Each person has their own caffeine tolerance. The caffeine you consume stays in your body for a day, and so if your sleep is not good, you might want to consider saying, "Bye-bye, caffeine," for a while. Cutting back, or kicking out caffeine is hard. If you are dependent on caffeine, it's going to suck, but reducing it or kicking it out may have a huge impact on your anxiety and can really help your sleep.

Kicking it out is not your only option, it's also worthwhile just to bring some more attention (and perhaps some caution) to it. Just be aware that it can throw your mood and worsen anxiety empowers you to make some changes around it. I like coffee, I have coffee sometimes, but I also know that if I've got a big presentation and I'm feeling anxious, I'm not going to have a coffee that day. My body can't handle it; I'll be through the roof, way more anxious about things. That's not a good day to have a coffee. Figure out for yourself when your body loves coffee and when you should be making another choice.

Packaged Foods

The last thing that I want to bring your attention to in this chapter is packaged foods. I know I brought this up a little bit when we talked about sugar and that your food that's packaged and processed often has a lot of sugar in it. It's important to be mindful about that from a blood sugar perspective. We also talked about the impact sugar has on your microbiome. But packaged food impacts the microbiome beyond its sugar content.

Prepackaged foods are designed not to have microbes grow on them. That's how they can sit in your pantry; they have preservatives in them. The job of the preservatives is to kill bacteria. Here's the problem, you aren't just made of body cells, you've got all your microbe friends that live in your digestive tract that help you.

So how does eating a packaged food with preservatives then impact them? Not surprisingly, it can disrupt them because it's anti-microbial. This is another reason you want to minimize the packaged foods in your diet and focus on more whole foods. I'm not saying, "never eat packaged food!" However, if there's a lot of packaged food in your diet, you should consider how that could be affecting your microbiome. Ask yourself if there are changes you could make to reduce the preservatives to help that gut flora thrive, to help it send great information back up to your brain.

More than anything, in this chapter, I want to bring some nuance. In nutrition, this debate is so often a black and white yelling match where everyone is screaming for their preferred perspective. "NEVER EAT PROCESSED FOOD. IT WILL KILL YOU" or "IT DOESN'T MATTER WHAT YOU EAT IT HAS NO IMPACT ON YOUR MOOD!" Obviously, neither of these things are true. Can you reduce your anxiety and improve your health by reducing sugar, alcohol, caffeine and processed foods - Yes. Do you have to be militant about it - No.

It's always your choice

The goal of this chapter is to empower you with the knowledge to a) make the choices you feel good about and b) provide some perspective about what's going on in your body so you can narrate your own experience differently.

Say you go to a wedding and decide you are going to enjoy some cake and champagne! How fun! Cheers! Congrats to the happy couple! Let's say that, after the party, you start to feel a little worried. You have healthy thoughts of "Hmmm, this is going quite late - I wonder how the kids are doing." These thoughts then spiral into the unhealthy territory of "We need to leave 10 minutes ago because the house is probably on fire." At this stage, it's worth also considering that "maybe this worry I'm having right now is worse because of what I ate, and the kids are probably fine."

Take Action ✐

Read your food labels. This week, read the labels on everything you eat. Get a better idea of how much sugar is in your diet and where it is coming from.

SLEEP

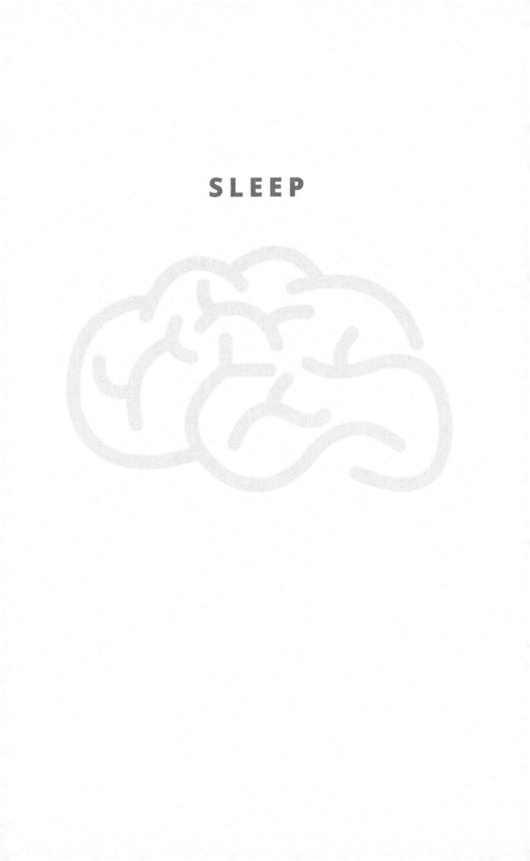

Chapter Eleven
YOU NEED A BEDTIME

HANDS UP IF YOU'VE GOT A BEDTIME.

If your hand is up - first - way to go. This section is going to be a breeze for you.

If your hand is not up, you are now in the category of "person who needs a bedtime" Contrary to popular belief, bedtimes are not just for children. They are magical tools that promote excellent sleep, no matter how old you are.

The Magic of Bedtimes

Bedtimes are magical because they harness the power of your own body to promote getting sleepy, being asleep and waking up refreshed in the morning. You see, your body has its own internal clock, a circadian rhythm that runs on a 24-hour clock. This clock runs your hormones that are responsible for being energetic and awake. So here's something you need to know about your hormones -they run best on routine. Every day your cortisol levels spike to get you out of bed in the morning and then slowly fall for the rest of the day. This is what is supposed to happen. By working with timing your sleep, you can harness your cortisol levels, so they are working for you! To do this, you've got to be consistent. Being consistent with your sleep is the best thing you can do to promote good sleep.

Why you need a good night's sleep

There is nothing like having a good night's sleep for your mental health. If you have ever struggled with insomnia, or if you suffered from depression after your baby was born that resolved when your baby started sleeping, you are probably thinking, "Obviously."

But sleep affects our mental health even in more subtle ways.

One of the things sleep does for us emotionally is it resets your emotional brain - the amygdala[18]. If you've noticed that you're more reactive and less able to respond to things, and you feel like you are WAY more emotional when you haven't had a good night's sleep - that's because it's true. Your limbic brain, your emotional brain, uses sleep to basically shut off and then turn back on again. If it hasn't had a chance to do that (at least six uninterrupted hours), it just still has all the activity from yesterday.

Think of it like a computer - it needs to be turned off, reset, and then turned back on not still to be running all the other stuff. You don't need to be running all the emotional programing from yesterday, on top of whatever today has in store for you. Knowing how important it is to get good sleep, let's talk about the three pieces that have to be in place for someone to get good sleep.

Pick a bedtime

Figure out when you need to get up in the morning to be able to do everything that you want to do in the morning and be where you need to be on time. Then work backwards to find a bedtime. So let's say you decide you need to get up at 6.30 to be able to do all the things that you need to do. Then count backwards from there and figure out how much sleep you need. Now I want you to think about how much sleep you're getting right now, but also what you think about how much sleep you need. Most people need eight hours of sleep. Some people need seven, and some people need nine. If you think that you need less than seven or more than nine, then I would encourage you to find a healthcare provider to sort that out with because you may need more support. On the higher end, it can be normal, but it usually isn't. If you think you need less than seven hours of sleep, take a minute to really consider what belief that's serving. Is it true that less than seven hours of sleep is where you do your very best work and is what your body actually needs?

I'm not saying there aren't people out there who are great on less sleep. I just don't think that it's as high as the number of people that tell me that they're fine on six hours of sleep. This is not the amount of sleep you need just to function and be "fine" I hope you are pushing for higher than "fine" You want to be optimal, right?

Sleep for your highest performance

How much sleep do you need to bring out your best self? Your least anxious, our highest functioning, most enthusiastic and authentic self? That takes great sleep, which in turn comes from a routine.

So grab that wake-up time, say 6:30, and count back, say 8 hours, to 10:30 - that becomes the bedtime. Then you can plan backwards from there to start getting ready for bed so you can be in bed falling asleep at your bedtime.

I encourage you to be consistent with your sleep routine. Even on the weekends. Even if you still have different start times for your job, and you start at different times on different days, you want to, as much as possible, have something that's routine, so your body knows what to expect. It works on a 24-hour clock. It likes consistency. And the more consistent you are with the sleep, the more your sleep will reward you with good quality sleep and feeling rested.

Take Action 🖉

How much sleep do you need? What consistent time are you going to set aside for your sleep window?

Chapter Twelve

NIGHT IS SUPPOSED TO BE DARK

HAVE YOU EVER BEEN CAMPING?

When I was 14, I was at a summer camp doing leadership training, and we went on an out trip. A dozen other teenagers and I canoed to an island where we set up tents in a clearing atop a hill. It was July in Ontario, and we had a beautiful, warm summer night. So, the group of us decided we were going to sleep outside on this smooth rock. I vividly remember sitting out there in our sleeping bags, chatting and looking at the stars. As the storytelling started winding down and the giggling got quiet, I was struck not just by how beautiful the whole thing was but by how dark it got and how quiet it was out on that Island with no electricity in sight.

This is how you were designed to experience sleep; in the dark and quiet.

Melatonin

Darkness is the key ingredient to melatonin, the hormone that regulates your sleep-wake cycle. If you think back to before the advent of electricity and electric lights, the world was a pretty dark place after the sun went down. In response to this darkness, your brain makes the hormone melatonin - and you get tired and fall asleep. In the morning, when the sun comes up, that light hits your eyes, and your brain starts to break apart the melatonin. That's the basis of the sleep-wake cycle: darkness.

Enter your cell phone, which, alongside all the other devices we have, computers, tablets, TVs and even streetlights, shine brightly into the hours and - let's be honest - minutes before we get ourselves to sleep. We have a big darkness deficit. There is not enough darkness in most of our evenings.

Give your phone a bedtime

Some other things you can do to promote darkness and good melatonin are to stay off your cell phone before you're going to sleep. I know there's apps and things that make it so it's not blue light. All that's great, and you can definitely start doing that as of 7:00 PM. But as of 20 minutes before you want to go to bed, aim for absolutely no screen time.

I often refer to this as your phone's bedtime (which should be before yours). Think of putting your phone to bed first, and then take care of whatever you're going to do in the evening to get yourself ready for bed. Having your cell phone physically away from your bed is important. If at all possible, put it out of your bedroom. Get an old-school alarm clock.

Phones are not great alarm clocks because the second that you look at them to check the time in the middle of the night, that light from the screen, starts breaking down your melatonin. It takes only three seconds, and your melatonin has decreased! You want to keep your melatonin so you can sleep, so put that cell phone far away from you!

Turn down the lights

The other way you can think about darkness is also to consider dimming the lighting in your house, starting around seven o'clock, or whenever the sun would be going down. You can use dimmer switches or turn off the bright overhead lighting and transition to softer lamplight. Anything that keeps you away from harsh light in the evening is going to help your body transition towards sleep.

To get better sleep, you need to get the light out of your bedtime and your bedtime routine. I want you to do everything that you can to make your room dark. You want to sleep in a cave reminiscent of time before electric lighting.

Take Action ✏

Take a tour of your bedroom. How dark is it? Check and see where light might be coming in. Do you have street light coming in through your window? Are there devices that you have? Do you have an alarm clock that has a light that shines in your eyes? Is there light coming from any other wireless routers that have little flashing lights?

Chapter Thirteen
QUIET MIND

THE LAST, AND FOR SOME OF YOU, THE MOST ELUSIVE PART TO A GOOD NIGHT'S sleep, is a quiet mind. I know this is a really big struggle for a lot of people with anxiety. The second your head hits the pillow, all the thoughts start racing. Just like the other parts of good sleep, this is something that can be addressed by encouraging good practices. You may need time before bed to do the work of organizing your thoughts.

Journalling
Journalling can be a helpful tool to organize thoughts before bed and let go of what's bothering you. Free flow journalling (where you just write whatever thoughts come into your head) can help some people let go of their day. Some people find journaling about emotional things get them worked up before they go to bed. It brings it all top of mind, and then they have difficulty sleeping. If that's true for you, don't do that kind of journaling. Try gratitude journaling instead, where you reflect on 3-5 great things that happened that day.

Planning
If your mind is busy with day to day activities before bed, you may want some more planning in your evening (and systems in your life). Try setting up tomorrow's to-do list before you go to sleep. This means that if you are lying in bed thinking, "Oh, I can't forget to get the dry cleaning! And I can't forget that Tommy needs $5 for hot lunch tomorrow!" or whatever it is that takes up that mental space and causes you not to be able to quiet the mind, create some time in your evenings to do and plan those things. There's always going to be things that need to get done tomorrow, and if you can pre-worry about them or pre-plan those things, you'll find it easier to quiet your mind at night.

Meditation
The other thing is to consider a mind quieting practice, such as breathing, prayer or meditation. We are going to dive deeper into meditation in a later chapter of this book. For now, think about implementing some of the breathing exercises from the earlier chapter as a practice right before you fall asleep. Later you can expand on that breathwork as you move towards growing your calming rituals.

Practice, Practice, Practice
It's important to remember that calming the mind before bedtime is a skill. You weren't born able to do it, and it takes practice to learn. Don't be frustrated if the first day you

journal, you go to bed, and you're like, "Well, I still thought of other things." It's just about practice. You didn't hop on a bike and start riding perfectly the first time you tried, and that's not going to happen with these practices either. Be consistent, keep practicing, and you will get better at them. Some days will be easier, and some will be harder - that's normal. So long as you are showing up for yourself, you are moving forward.

Creating a Bedtime Routine

All right, so now that we have talked through melatonin, calming the mind, and having a bedtime routine, I want you to take some time to write out your awesome bedtime ritual, to think about what it would be like to have time dedicated to you to prepare yourself for sleep. How does that ritual look?

It might involve meditation; it might involve turning down the lights; it may involve some sort of personal hygiene; it may involve charging your electronics and putting them to bed. I just want you to think about it and structure that out. Maybe all of those things happen in a 30-minute window, or maybe it starts sooner. Maybe your bedtime routine starts before you even get home from work, and it starts with thinking about and then writing down all the activities that you know need to be dealt with when you go in the next day, so you don't have to bring any of that home with you. Then they aren't keeping you up at night, and you can turn off your work phone. Maybe your sleep routine needs to start as early as that, or maybe when it comes to 10:00, you just want to meditate, put your phone away, brush your teeth, wash your face, and go to bed. It's whatever YOU need.

Take Action ✏

Write out your new bedtime routine like it's a prescription to you from you.

EXERCISE

Chapter Fourteen
JOYFUL MOVEMENT

I NEVER THOUGHT OF MYSELF AS AN ATHLETE.

Growing up, I was that clumsy, nerdy kid who was always walking into things. My lack of coordination was deeply concerning to my gym-teacher father. From a young age, he was always trying to help me improve my physical coordination and agility.

I was so uncoordinated I couldn't stop a ball from hitting me in the face. To ensure I could learn this skill - and not cry in the process - my dad took me to Canadian Tire[19] and threw the kids' toy balls at my face. When they hit me in the face (because of course, they did) if I didn't cry, the ball was soft enough, and we took it home to practice.

My mother would jest "When it comes to athletics your father's genes are superior, but mine are dominant."

I played soccer every summer of my childhood - I don't think I ever scored a goal in a game.

I stopped taking gym classes as soon as I could in high school. And while I joined the gym one semester in university, I think I went twice I felt so out of my league with all the equipment, with no idea what I was doing and no one to show me how, I quickly gave up.

I wasn't athletic.

I told myself that for years. Then one day, I found the courage to question if it was really true. Am I not athletic? Or am I limiting myself with the belief that "I am not athletic"?

Spoiler alert, you don't have to be a world-class athlete to be athletic. For years I had been trying out different activities – yes, in fits and spurts. I would do yoga for months only to turn around and go a year without stepping into the studio. My husband and I would play in a rec league and not go back for the next season. I'd start running for a summer and then stop halfway through.

Slowly, over time, I learned what activities I enjoyed and how to keep myself doing them more and more regularly. At my best, I was on my yoga mat 3x per week, playing ultimate frisbee every week and walking 5km a day - and I was doing all that and telling myself, "you aren't athletic."

---

[19]Canadian Tire is a Canadian outdoor all-purpose store for everything from gardening tools, sports equipment and (obviously) tires

I had to let go of the idea that being an active person meant I had to run races like my mom did or lift super heavy things like friends I admire do. Being athletic became less about the outcome and more about the actions. Less about meeting anyone else's expectations about how I should move my body and more about finding out what makes me happy, and my body feel good.

So that is what we are going to talk about for you. Specifically, this chapter is about exercise and moving your body in ways that are fun and that you enjoy.

How Much Movement

The goal is first to get you moving more than you are and then to get you to a place where you're moving as much as you would like to. If you really press me for how often, I recommend daily movement. Your body loves it, and it's really great for your mental health. That does not mean you need to be going to the gym for an hour every day; I want to like dispel that myth right away, but I do mean some kind of movement.

If you are a gym rat and you are going to the gym every day, and you love it, good for you! I say this with 100% sincerity - that is awesome. Keep it up!

Why Move?

Exercise is an amazing mood booster. We know from research it is an excellent treatment for both depression and anxiety[20]. Most people think exercise is good for mood because of the endorphins that get released from exercise. This happy sensation, sometimes called a runner's high, is one of the ways exercise supports mood.

But the full benefits of increasing physical activity come twelve weeks into an exercise program.

Exercise is really great for your overall nervous system and your cardiovascular health. It's important to think of heart health when we think of brain health because they are connected. We need a healthy cardiovascular system to get good blood flow going to our brains and to supports brain health.

All our body systems are connected. Just like we need good food and digestion to get all the good nutrients up to our brain, we need to have good physical activity to get the nutrients from our body up to our brain as well.

The other piece is that exercise helps us is with growing new neurons and new neural pathways. When you exercise, your brain and skeletal muscle produce BDNF - brain-derived neurotrophic factor[21]. BDNF helps your neural plasticity. We used to think only the brain made this compound, but it's also made in the brain and the muscles by exercising! This is really amazing because your movement is something you can control. You don't have to wait on your brain to make this or accept that your brain isn't making enough on its own. You can encourage its development with your actions.

How to Stick with it

There is a key ingredient in an exercise plan that gets missed sometimes - you have to love what you do. Think about anytime you moved your body, and it made you smile. Maybe you were dancing in your kitchen; maybe you were finishing a really hard run; maybe you were mastering a new yoga pose. Maybe you were lifting something extremely heavy, and you felt like, "I'm so strong." Whatever it was, think about that: what were you doing, what do you enjoy, and start a list.

Whenever I give this homework, there is always someone who looks at me and says, "I don't like to move my body. I've never done anything fun moving my body. I don't even know what that would look like." If you're feeling that way right now, don't get discouraged, you are not alone in this feeling. What you're going to do instead is make a list of things that you think might be fun to try. It doesn't matter if you have ever done them. If you've never done them and you don't have any like negative thoughts towards them, that's probably a good place to start! Brainstorm a list of anything you might like to do.

Take Action ✐

Write a list of ways to move your body that you like to do and/or things you'd like to try.

Chapter Fifteen

BALANCING YOUR EXERCISE: PEACEFUL PAUSES AND POWER PUSHES

The Energy of Movement

When it comes to the energy of exercise, not all activity is created equal. Like all things, activity is made of yin and yang energy. Yin is considered to be more feminine energy. It has more substance, slower-moving, colder and calming. Yang energy is considered to be more masculine, higher energy, it moves faster; it feels hotter and more energizing. Everything has yin and yang; they need each other.

It can be helpful to think of exercise through this model of yin and yang, Peaceful Pauses, and Power Pushes. Depending on how we engage in an activity and what type of activity we do, we can create a very different feeling in the body. A Peaceful Pause physical activity is something that's restorative. It's typically slower-moving and more of a relaxation experience. Think of swimming laps gently in a pool or going for a quiet walk in the forest. A Power Push activity is more exertion based. Your heart rate goes up; you experience heat in the body; you may feel excited or energized during or after the activity.

Go back to those so with those types of activities that you've gone through and made that list of, it's time to start thinking about sorting them into whether this is a Peaceful Pause (Yin) or a Power Push (yang) activity.

What makes something a peaceful pause or a power push?

Let's talk about yoga. A yoga practice can be one, the other or both, and it can depend on who you are and how you practice. Does yoga get your heart rate up? Do you leave it feeling energized? If so, then that type of yoga that you're doing that gives you those things, that's a power push. Whereas if your yoga class is more slow-moving, you hold poses for a long time, you end up feeling a lot more relaxed after yoga and not so amped up. That's more of a peaceful pause yoga.

Another example that I use is hiking. If you go for a mindful hike and you're meandering around, you're looking at the birds, and you're just enjoying nature - not in a rush - that's a peaceful pause. If you are out for a hike and you climb up boulders, and your breath has gone up as you feel those gluts pushing yourself up the hill, that's a power push. A hike could be a mostly peaceful or mostly powerful activity, and maybe you went for a hike where you did both! You did some super intense stuff, and then you also did some calm stuff. These are not rules.

As you look through your own activities, start to figure out if they are more energizing or more calming, a more peaceful experience or more powerful. Probably you'll find most activities, just like all of us and everything in the world, have both of those energies to them. But it is still worth separating them out. This becomes important when we start to plan physical activity.

Now that you've got your list of activities, it's time to start putting them into your week.

Balancing Peaceful Pauses and Power Pushes

In general, as we age, we need more peaceful pauses in our activity compared with power pushes. Think of the last time you were around a young child. They have this ability - and this need - to run around all day, they can go, go, go, go, go. In traditional Chinese Medicine, this is explained by saying children have "excess yang." This energy needs to get out so children can grow up. As we age, we just don't have that as much yang anymore! So it's important to balance that out with more calming and gentle activities.

Now the other important thing is your energy reserves. If you have been through chronic illness, so meaning you've been treated for a serious illness, maybe you've got an irritable bowel disease, or you've survived cancer, those things really deplete your energy. So you may need to do more peaceful pauses than power pushes, even if you're a younger person. Be mindful of your health status, what your energies are, what's getting depleted and what needs to be built up.

Stress also decreases our energy. We may need to do more peaceful pauses for activity in the earlier stages of a new exercise plan. This increases your stamina and ability. Think of any couch to 5K plan. You don't start by running the 5K! This would be very much a power push activity. You start with mostly walking (peaceful) with a few short power push sprints put in there. This is how you should think of your activity in general.

I use this technique with my patients and myself if I've been away from exercise for a little while. I always add more peaceful pauses in, before I add in more power pushes. Because I know that's helpful for me. It helps improve my physical fitness to the point where I can do more of the power pushes and not be exhausted, throw up, or injure myself.

Schedule it Out

Think of what balance might be right for you and schedule it out. Plan out your ideal week and then think about where you were at last week and create a bridge plan to move you from where you are to where you want to be. If last week you went for one walk and what you've put on your activity list is to go for three hikes and do three yoga classes, create a plan to increase your activity gradually until you hit your goal. Add one thing this week, and then increase by one activity per week until you reach your full plan. This week you do one hike and one yoga class, next week you do two yoga classes and a hike, the week after you do two hikes and two yoga classes. In a few weeks, you will have built up your stamina and be on your way to the full power of the medicine that is movement.

Make sure that you are setting aside the time in your schedule for WHEN you are going to exercise. Saying you are going to hike "this week" probably won't happen - there is always tomorrow. Scheduling to leave work at 4:30 on Tuesday to go to the conservation area and hike for an hour makes it much more likely to happen.

Take Action ✎

Write down your exercise plan using activities you love and balancing your power pushes and peaceful pauses for your age, fitness and current level of activity. Schedule them into your day timer or set calendar reminders on your smartphone to follow through with your plan.

MINDFULNESS

Chapter Sixteen

NON-JUDGMENTAL AWARENESS

I WAS SITTING IN THE BALCONY AT CHURCH, EXPECTING A TYPICAL ACADEMIC sermon that Sunday morning. When the words "Imagine you are in the hospital…" came out of the pulpit, I knew that's not where things were headed.

As I listened to the scene offered for my imagination, with the strange sounds and blinking lights of hospital machines, there was nothing 'imaginary' about the scene forming in my mind. My mind was right back at my brother's bedside in the critical care unit of the hospital.

Hot tears welled up in my eyes and, in a blink, began streaming down my face.

The pain and sadness at that moment felt as real and raw as the first time I walked into that hospital ward. I wanted it to stop.

One thought crystallized in my mind: "I don't want to be doing this right now."

I got up and walked out. I sat confused on the stairs. I went to the kitchen and got some water. Wandered around to see if the Sunday School was ok - Maybe they needed me to do something? Anything to avoid the pain and surprise of being pulled into that feeling.

I felt anxious and lost.

I was avoiding what was happening right then, both inside myself (the pain and sadness) and externally (with no awareness or attention to the building I was in or my current surroundings).

I wish I could tell you that I grounded myself, realized it was OK to be upset, got support for my feelings and moved on with my day. Some days I do achieve that, but not this day.

The second church ended, I grabbed my family and got out of the building as quickly as possible.

Later, on reflection, I could see that what made this more difficult was not the experience or even the sad thoughts – that had happened before, and I'd been fine. It was that my expectation (an academic sermon) was different than my reality (an emotional experience) and that I was focused on wishing things were different rather than accepting where they are.

The attempt to avoid where I was at that moment, what I was truly thinking and feeling - that is what caused my suffering.

This is true for many of my patients.

"What's the worst part of your anxiety?" I ask

"This isn't really me." "I don't feel like myself." "I just get so frustrated." "I shouldn't feel this way," They say.

This avoidance of what is really happening adds a layer of pain and discomfort to the current reality. This is when I start to bring up mindfulness, and often the eye-rolls start.

"I've tried meditation, and I'm just not good at it." "I can't just sit there." "No - you don't get it; I can't meditate."

This is when we start to back things up - a lot. So if you hate meditation come on and roll back to the beginning with me and see if my reframe works for you, as it has for meditation haters before you.

What is Mindfulness
The definition of mindfulness that I like is bringing non-judgmental awareness to the present moment. And I think that that's worth breaking down. First is this whole non-judgmental part.

Understanding Non-Judgement
Non-judgmental means that we're reserving (or let's be honest - working on reserving) our judgements or decisions about what's happening. So often, when we do something or when we think something, we add in some colour to our thoughts in the form of judgement. We say that's good, or that's bad, or some variation of "I like that" or "This sucks." Mindfulness, at its core, is just about challenging ourselves not to make judgements all the time. It's moving away from this binary thinking, where we say this goes in this box or this box. This is good, and that is bad.

We want just to move away from that and replace it with "this is."

So maybe in the past, you've felt anxious, and you've said to yourself, "Oh no, I'm feeling anxious." The "oh no" part is judging it! You are saying, "it's bad to be anxious." When we practice mindfulness, we work on removing the judgment piece. So, "I am anxious," becomes just that - being anxious - without saying it's bad to be anxious. In this way, we lose the added pain of the story of our experience and just sit where you are.

The present moment
The second part of that definition goes into more of where you are to direct your non-judgmental attention, and that is to the present moment. What's happening right now? Right now, you are reading this book. You might be reading in on some kind of device, and you are probably sitting on something. Maybe there are people around you. You can probably hear sounds if you pay attention. When you do this, you stop thinking about what happened yesterday, or five minutes ago, and are fully present in the moment.

Practicing non judgement

I remember when he was getting ready for this party. And I was looking through my closet, and I just had no idea what I was going to wear to it as I wasn't sure what other people were going to wear. I hadn't been to an event quite like this one before. I was going through my closet, flipping back and forth on what I was going to do. And I had this epiphany. "If everyone else at this event is even half as worried about what they are wearing as I am worried about what I'm wearing right now, no one will have any space in their head even to process what I've bothered to put on my body." No one cares. It was so freeing. I put on whenever I wanted, and I went to the party.

At that moment, I realized that I cared more about what I thought about me than what everybody else thought about me. We get into these judgmental states.

The question becomes, who are you really judging?

All judgment is self-judgment. All criticism is self-criticism. If you say "they are too loud" what you're really saying is, "I'm afraid that I'm too loud." The only person that's being held back by that is you. It's your light, your spark. That could be a gift in this world that you are denying. What could you create? What good would you bring, what legacy could you leave? Could you make something that actually matters? If you just stopped judging?

Building this awareness

This is the basis around this mindfulness piece and where we are going to build out mindfulness practices from. Anytime you read the word mindful or mindfulness, remember this is all about bringing non-judgmental awareness about what's happening right now - in this moment.

Chapter Seventeen
MEDITATION

MINDFULNESS MEDITATION IS ONE WAY TO CULTIVATE A FORMAL MINDFULNESS practice. In this way, you set aside time each day to meditate or to engage in mindful practices like mindful breathing. I really encourage you to give a formal mindfulness meditation a try even if you don't end up with meditation as the way you practice mindfulness most often in your life.

To be successful with meditation, like nutrition, sleep and exercise before, you need a plan. So, in order to set yourself up for a trial of meditation, you need to decide when, where, and how you're going to meditate. Really, these are decisions that you can make for yourself. The most important thing is to really make them.

Find a time
First, commit to a time. Pick a time where you're going to meditate. Times when people often are successful at implementing a meditation practise are first thing in the morning and before bed. I schedule both of these into my day and usually hit one of them. This is my reality of having a young child - no matter how early I get up to meditate - sometime she gets up before or during that time.

Pick a place
Next, pick where you are going to meditate. I usually meditate on the couch at my house. That's just my favourite spot. But you may find a different spot. Picking a spot to meditate can be helpful because then when you go to that spot - it's time to meditate. It helps your neural pathways and enhances your practice.

Find a tool
Then the last part is to think about how to meditate. If you've had previous mindfulness training, you may already have a plan as to how you like to meditate. If that's you - awesome. For the rest of us, it's usually more helpful to have some guidance.

There are a variety of guided meditation resources out there.

A lot of my patients like the convenience of learning from an app. Headspace. Calm. Ohm. Stop Think Breathe. Insight Timer. These are all free or paid apps that will teach you / guide you through meditations.

YouTube is another great resource. Some of my patients really just love finding different meditations on YouTube to listen to. I would just encourage you that once you've set it up, don't watch the screen. Put that away, put some headphones in or have it playing but closed. So you're not getting the visual information, you're just getting the sounds.

Take Action 🖉

Create a plan for when, where and how you are going to try out a formal meditation practice.

Chapter Eighteen
MINDFUL LIVING

GROWING UP, NO ONE BUT MY DAD WAS ALLOWED TO CUT THE GRASS. I remember watching him from the deck as he meticulously cut our lawn - the same pattern every time. He would go around the edges of the flower beds and then cut back and forth in a diagonal pattern, never missing a blade of grass between passes. His speed was constant. The roar of the lawnmower, the smell of gasoline mixed with freshly mown grass; even now, this reminds me of my dad.

I avoided interrupting him while he was mowing the lawn at all costs, even if the phone was for him. Between the noise and his focused determination, it was hard to get his attention, but also, there was this feeling like I had interrupted something important. Like I'd disturbed the flow and broken the magic.

Looking back on it now, cutting the lawn was probably a meditation for my dad.

You see, formal meditation is not the only way to bring mindfulness into your life, and in this chapter, we are going to cover some of the other ways to bring that non-judgmental awareness into your day to day life

Exercise
One of the places you can bring your full nonjudgmental awareness is to your exercise. When you want to be mindful in exercise, instead of working out with music or listening to a podcast, you actually just spend some time while you are exercising, bringing your full attention to your body. You begin to focus on what's going on in your body as you move and pay attention to the environment that you are exercising in and just working on being fully present in the moment.

If you come across some thoughts while exercising, you don't need to ruminate on them. You can just say, "Okay, thank you. I'm running right now." and then go back to focusing on your breath, focusing on how your muscles feel, how it feels in your body to be moving in this way. You can do this for all or part of your exercise.

Eating
Another area you can bring mindfulness to is eating. There are a couple of different reasons why you might want to do this.

One - it's a really great mindfulness practice. All the benefits of mindfulness, the increased focus, increased attention, decreased depression, anxiety, decreased pain, all of those benefits, come from mindfulness practices in general, and that includes mindful eating.

The other thing is that it really helps your digestion. When you bring in that mindfulness and pay attention to what you are eating, your conscious brain is more engaged in your digestion.

Chores

Another fun way to bring mindfulness into your life, and to maybe make some things that are kind of unenjoyable a little bit more fun, is to bring mindfulness into household chores. You know "mindful dishes" and "mindful sweeping" and even "mindful laundry." Of all those things, my favourite is mindful laundry.

I know it sounds ridiculous, but I love hanging up clothes. I love sorting them, looking at the colours, and when I hang them up, it's a really mindful activity for me. I feel like everything else kind of goes away - it's just me - and the laundry.

When I was a kid, we used to have a big long clothesline in our back yard, and I used to try and see how many clothes pegs I needed, and I would just focus on that. And even now, when I'm laying out the clothes on my drying rack at home, I'm thinking, where will they all fit? Sometimes I arrange them by colour, and I just get really focused on what the fabric feels like and where they are all going to hang.

Of all the chores that's one that resonates most with me, but I encourage you to whatever activities that you have going on today, whether that's washing dishes, whether that's sweeping floors, whether that's hanging laundry, to try what it's like to bring your nonjudgmental awareness to that activity, that mindful attitude.

When you're washing the dishes, rather than listening to music or planning out what you're going to do the next day, work on being engaged in what you're actually doing. How does the soap feel? What does it smell like? Is the water hot or cold? What's the texture of the dishcloth? What's the texture of the dishes? Just get as much sensory information about the present moment as you can.

Much the same thing applies to that activity of sweeping. Feeling that pressure of the broom in your hand, feeling your arm muscles as you move through sweeping exercises. What is that pressure like? What's that movement like? Just be as involved as possible when thoughts come in about what else you need to do other than sweeping the floor to make your house clean. Just letting those go and in the moment, just focusing on the act of moving that broom. And that's really a way that you can incorporate some mindfulness mindset into some of the different activities that you might need to do around chores.

Hobbies

The last thing before we move on from mindfulness, let's talk about mindful hobbies. Consider whether you have a hobby where mindfulness is a part of that or could be a part of that. Anything, any hobby or activity that brings your attention to the present moment is something that could be done mindfully.

The classic example of a mindful hobby is colouring. Colouring has been shown to create very similar neural pathways to meditating. It's the closest hack; if you're really struggling with setting up a meditation practice, I encourage you to keep trying, but you also may want to incorporate some mindful colouring.

A lot of people get a lot of benefit from colouring. I think this is why there's been this explosion of adult colouring books in recent years, is that they promote a meditative brain pattern, and they can be beneficial because of that. And so, if you don't have a hobby that you feel is calming and helps you get into a meditative state, I would definitely encourage you to try colouring.

However, before you try colouring, take some time and check if there's something that you are doing right now already that functions the same way for you. Some people knit or craft or make art in a way that already fills this role. If you have something like that, try creating without doing or listening to something else, and practice bringing your full attention to the crafting.

Making is not limited to what we traditionally think of as crafts. For some people, working on their cars is a meditative process and really pulls them into the present moment. Really, they're not thinking about anything else except for that mechanical repair. It's really not about what kind of art or creative project you are working on. I think any kind of art or creativity can function in this mindful way.

If you have something that you have in your life you know pulls you into a mindful space, ask yourself if you have enough time and enough space to do it as much as your heart needs to. If not, can you make more time for it? If you don't have something that falls into a mindful hobby - try colouring.

Take Action ✏

This week, bring non-judgmental awareness into your day to day activities. Challenge yourself to try using mindfulness in chores and exercise. Make time to enjoy a hobby mindfully.

CONNECTION

Chapter Nineteen
KNOWING YOURSELF

HAVE YOU EVER HAD A MOMENT SO PERFECT YOU JUST WANTED TO LOCK IT IN?
A moment of pure bliss and tranquility, where you felt timeless?

One summer and I was performing in an opera that took place in the middle of the woods. Yes, I know its unusual, stay with me. When I look back at the three weeks I spent living in a cabin and singing in the woods the whole thing seems magical.

Locked into my mind is one of the few "days off" we had. I spread out a towel on the grass behind the cabin I was staying in, grabed my discman and a bar of chocolate and completely imersed myself in my senses.

Years later I can still go back there in my minds eye. I can feel the hot sun on my body. The taste and feel of the chocolate melting in my mouth. Hear my favourite song from the CD I listened to that summer.

While delightful, none of those things is what makes this memory so potent. It's that in that moment, how ever long it was, there was only this. I had no fears, no anxieties because I was just completely at one, with myself, who I was, what I was doing and with nature / God / the divine. It was all there, all one, in that moment.

When I talk about connection, this is what I mean.

I mean connecting to the pure divine presence inside each of us.

I mean connecting to the divine in ourselves and then looking outward and seeing it - in every flower, every tree, every child, every stranger, in our friends and families, our partner, the people we disagree with and our own reflection in the mirror, our own physical body.

Beyond the biology
The first part of this book has focused on the biologic underpinnings of anxiety. We have talked about the things you can do to set up your brain and nervous system to foster a calm physical and emotional state. But this has not addressed the root cause of anxiety. Anxiety, in its deepest sense, appears when we have a deep, deep down disconnection from the conscious knowing of who we are. Of course, deep down, you always know who you are, but there is a lot of pain from not knowing, or more accurately feeling like you don't know.

There is the pain and anxiety in not knowing and also when we know who we are, but we are unable to express it fully. The inability to fully be our true selves and who we know we are creates dis-congruence in our mind, body and spirit and causes an immense amount of pain and disease.

Being in a place of "I know who I am, but I just can't be, do, have, or say that right now," is incredibly painful.

Your true identity, who you truly are, when that gets put out front, and you can be that person, that creates a sense of ease. There is security in being who you are that decreases the anxiety that comes with the alternative of wearing a mask. When you're wearing a mask, there's always this worry that someone might see past it, or that you might slip and the mask will fall off, and someone will see what's underneath.

True identity and masks

When it comes to putting ourselves out there and moving through the world, we often don a mask. There's a lot of different ways to do that and a lot of different reasons that we do it. These masks also have a lot of variation. But one of the reasons that we do this is as a form of protection of our innermost selves, our most vulnerable self.

Wearing a figurative mask means that what we put out there for others to see is something that we've fabricated. It's external, built on top of a piece of our identity, rather than showing the gooey sticky vulnerable thing that's inside. This let's us "save face" if someone doesn't like it. If someone says, "you don't belong here." Or, "You need to shut up." "You need to get out." If we are wearing a mask, then we can tell ourselves, "That's not really me." And so we develop these masks for different situations as a way of protecting that vulnerability of being seen.

But the problem with that is that being seen is one of our core drivers. We want to both be seen and belong.

And our deepest fear is that we will be seen and rejected.

And so by saving ourselves from being seen, we save ourselves the pain of someone rejecting the parts of ourselves we hold most dear.

Wearing a mask offers a certain level of protection, yet it comes with its own anxieties. You see, the mask might slip. And we are so afraid when we're wearing a mask that someone will see through it and see what's underneath that.

We've been wearing some of our masks so long that we don't know where we stop, and the mask starts. Part of this work in identity is starting to pull apart the questions of "what's me, and what masks have I been wearing?" One of those is performative. And one of these is mine. As I mentioned at the start of this chapter, I come from a theatre background. My degree, before science and nutrition, is actually in theatre studies. And there's this interesting play between being onstage and offstage - pulling on the persona of the character that you need to be, and then taking it off again. This is a challenging thing to do. We hear of these Hollywood method actors where they step into this character that they're playing so fully 'playing' them day and night, onset and off, so that they no longer have to go through the difficult process of slipping this mask on and off. They've refined this skill that the rest of us do in our daily lives as we switch roles.

Depending on our backgrounds and our environments, we may have to switch roles more often than someone else. It's hard. It's anxiety-provoking, because what if we put the wrong face on the more spaces that allow authentic expression. The more we can show up without having to wear some kind of mask, the less anxious this world is going to be. The anxiety of this mask is because of the dissonance. The internal dissonance between holding out something that we're not, and holding something behind it that we are, just hoping that we do a good enough job to fool everyone in the situation. Perhaps we might even be trying to fool ourselves.

Masks and Privilege

My life experience with this has not been as challenging as the experiences of other people. I have many privileges not the least of them being that I have not lived somewhere where just being my most authentic self would cause a threat to my life. Everyone should be afforded the oppourtunity to step into the full expression of themselves - without fear of retribution. There are systemic reasons why this is not the case right now and it is essential to our collective peace and freedom that we fight for a more inclusive world. We need to uproot discrimination in all forms - racism, classism, sexism, homophobia, Islamophobia, anti-semitism, all of these things and more that prevent each person on this planet exist in their skin safely and with their full humanity expressed. These prejudices create mandatory masks. This is why respecting safe spaces is so important; they create environments where people do not have to wear a mask. How do we create more of that? I don't think I have the answers here, at least not at the social scale; I'm not an expert on that. But we need to move away from this dissonance into congruence. We have to create an environment where masks are not needed, where people are safe to take them off. And then we as mask-wearers have to be brave enough to take off our masks and expose our gooey center.

How we take off the mask

So what do we need to take off the mask? First, we have to feel safe enough to be seen. Otherwise, the pain of not being seen, however deep it is, cannot be overcome. Our brains will choose our safety first as an issue of our survival. This will happen until either we create the conditions for safety or the pain of being unseen becomes so unbearable that we risk our safety (real or imagined) to be be seen.

As previously stated, some of this safety is external and some is internal. In this section we are going to focus on internal validation and self-esteem. How can we fortify our sense of self so we have the courage to risk being known and the possibility of rejection? How do we get to the point where we are ok with ourselves, so it's ok if others don't like us or our choices?

Let's start with where we get our validation for our personality, for who we are and our self-worth. Is it coming from an internal source, or is it coming from an external source? This is the part where you might expect me to say that you have to love yourself. That all of your validation has to come from the inside out. Well, that would be great. However, we're not all built that way. So I'm going to say that it's okay to want it from the outside. Go for it, ask for it, work for it and enjoy it. With the caveat that you can't base your entire self worth on it.

You have to insulate yourself from the fact that not everyone's going to like you, and that's okay. Insulate yourself by building an interior sense of self-worth that says, "I am valuable. I am Beloved. I belong. Just as I am."

How I found my internal self worth

I always hesitate to go into the messier portions of this. In my own mind, I say, "Okay, this is a great idea Katie. But how do we then go about cultivating this internal self-belief? This idea that I am intrinsically good intrinsically valuable - how do we find that?" And I always stop, because I truthfully, don't know how you are going to find it.

However, I do know how I find it. It is my hope that by sharing a bit of how I go there, you will see and be open to options for you to do the same. The main reason I hesitate because I don't want to evangelize. Your path is entirely yours, and when it comes to spirituality and spiritual growth, I truly believe there are as many paths as there are people. I'm sharing this with the hope that you will see past the parts of my journey that are mine alone to the possibilities that may be on your own path.

I found this internal validation in my faith through divine love, through Christ consciousness.

I was at the hospital. My brother was in the critical Intensive Care Unit. I was sitting by a window in the sunshine, feeling the sun on my face. I felt peaceful, not alone. I felt a universal love that filled me with awe and wonder toward the world around me. Knowing that experience existed, knowing there was such a state as that – it changed my life. It moved me in a direction that I wanted to spend more time in. Filled with that love and peace, there is no anxiety. There's a deep comfort of "This has always been." Of "You have always been taken care of and will always be taken care of. You don't need to be afraid." This sort of feeling reminds me that I'm loved even when I'm wrong, that I'm inherently good even when I make mistakes, or do something that I shouldn't have done. That I'm not a bad person.

This kind of compassion changed how I was able to see myself but also how I saw others. The beauty of this world, from that state, is like the way different faces of friends and strangers just fill you with delight. Each face, its own beautiful, divine image. I think this is what people talk about when I talk about seeing God in the faces of others. It's people, but it's also buildings and plants and music and art. It all just seems so miraculous and gorgeous.

I'm still learning to intentionally move into this place how to spend more time here. I am still learning how to make more decisions from this zone. I am still learning how to act from a place of universal love. And, like everything we've talked about in this book, I bring this up not to talk about being perfect or aim for some sort of perfect monastic life where we're all operating from the state of love at all times. I also explicitly want to avoid the shame that exists within my religious tradition of Christianity where mental health issues get ignored and undertreated because they are "a sign of lack of faith" While experiencing faith, awe and wonder are medicine for anxiety, a lack of faith is not an appropriate 'cause' of this (or frankly any other) disease.

What happens when we start stringing these moments together? What happens when we strive for more and create more intentionality, more peace, and more love? What happens when we keep coming back and returning to this state? How does that change us? How does that change our leadership? How does that change this world? This is a beautiful thing to imagine.

Identity

When we start to peel off figurative masks and sort out what parts of our identity is truly us we can begin to wonder "who am I". We have spent the first part of this book addressing your physical body. While you have a body, it is not all of what many consider makes us. You have feelings. You are spirit. Just as your body communicates their physical needs to you - your spirit energy communicates with you as well. You can connect with this by dedicating time to connect with yourself.

Learning to tune inwards

You may find it easier to begin by listening to your body, which is very wise and already knows what you need. Your body asks you for things all the time. The question is not "can my body speak to me" but "do you hear what it is saying" Bodies ask for food, water, exercise and sex. They might ask for more quiet or more company. More excitement or more peace. They tell you when something hurts and when something feels wonderful. Are you listening?

Every day, my husband gets home from work and hardly says hi to me because he has to run to the bathroom and go pee. Now, I understand his job is busy there's a lot of things that happen in a day, but there's a part of me that wonders, have you not paid attention to that all day? Did you not hear those whispers?

I'm not just blaming him - I do this too. At times I get to the end of a busy day seeing patients, and I notice, "I didn't eat enough." I feel kind of cold and worn out, and like my brain can't focus properly.

Imagine in a day where you're hopping from thing to thing - in and out of different meetings. Have you ever reached the end of your day and gone, "crap, I forgot to pour myself some water today!"

With so many distractions, how do we create that space to listen and reconnect with ourselves? I had the pleasure of hearing Dr. Aviva Romm speak live at a conference in my first year of clinical practice. Dr. Romm talked about giving ourselves "permission to pause." This is intentionally giving ourselves space to stop, turn inwards, and ask, "what do I need right now? What's my body telling me?"

In an ideal world, we are in constant communication with our bodies, and we know what our bodies need all the time. Realistically, most of us (myself included) are still learning to pay attention amongst the many obligations and distractions of work, parenthood and modern life. But there is no need to try and do this on our own, and I encourage you to think of what you can use as prompts or reminders throughout your day.

One of the techniques that I use in my practice is I have my patients create phone alarms or calendar alarms for "biology breaks" at specific times in their day. When the alarm goes off, they take it as a reminder to stop, take a couple of breaths, and check in with their body and see what it might need.

Listening to your feelings

While connecting with your body is a great start, you are not just a physical body. Your feelings and emotions are a part of you. To engage with these in the way of connection and union to self in a way that alleviates our deepest fears and anxieties, we need to bring in the attitude of non-judgmental awareness you've been cultivating through your mindfulness practice.

Now seems like a good spot to point out there are no "bad" feelings. In fact, all the great teachers and gurus have all repeated that there is no suffering from feelings, even the negative ones. The suffering comes from not expressing your feelings or from wishing they were different. By creating space for all - and I mean all - emotion, we remove the pain and anxiety of needing things to be any different than they are at this moment.

So how do we connect with our emotions? This is an important question, and it's something that gets overlooked in our culture. While growing up, each of us was taught about our emotions - sometimes directly, often indirectly. Depending on our culture, we may have been taught that certain emotions were more or less acceptable for us to have or to express. Remember this, and know it's okay if it's a little difficult at the beginning to identify your true feelings.

An example of this is feeling sad and feeling angry. Often girls are socialized into expressing more sadness, and that's considered acceptable. Boys are often told to "man up" or that boys don't cry. This is incredibly harmful to people of all genders.

The gender imbalance in anxiety

'Man up' - a phrase that masks anxiety and creates anxiety. This phrase is hurting people, no matter what their gender. One of my issues with conversations around anxiety is that there's a lot of groups out there claiming this as a women's health problem. This is because more women than men are diagnosed with anxiety. But this does not make it a women's health problem. Yes, it affects women. And that's important. But it's also important that this affects men and is under-diagnosed in men. To me, the problem is not that so many women are being diagnosed with anxiety. The problem is that so many men aren't – even though they are struggling with it. What is happening to these men? How are they falling through the cracks?

To me, this is the reverse of a cautionary tale of heart disease. For a long time, heart attacks were considered mainly a "men's health problem." Even now, we miss heart attacks in women because the way that they experience a cardiovascular incident doesn't look like the way it shows up in men. This is a very practical difference. And all of our research and understanding into what it means to have a heart attack is based around that core group we began investigating in, namely, men. So when you think of a heart attack, you think of chest pain and shooting pain down the left arm and numbness into the jaw.

But in women, this is not the most common presentation of a heart attack. Women are more likely to have abdominal symptoms than arm-focussed symptoms, and because of that, we miss Heart attacks in women, and women die because of this.

This is, I fear, what is happening with anxiety in men. Much of our research and historical understanding of anxiety has focused on women. Much of this has focused on behaviours stereotyped as being feminine. I am referring to the overthinking, the panic, the hyperventilation. Everything we know about anxiety and how anxiety most commonly presents is actually how anxiety most commonly presents in women. Anxiety is not a women's disease. It just looks different in men.

We know this for a couple of reasons. First, it's impossible to talk about gender and sex bias in medicine and in diagnosing anxiety without looking at our culture. From a young age - from boyhood – men are denied the expression of their feelings. Phrases like boys don't cry, and telling young boys to man up when they cry, are hurtful. These things prevent boys from learning the emotional skills and the emotional intelligence that they need to be able to find peace with themselves, to be in a relationship, to manage themselves in the workplace.

When the only allowed emotion is anger, all emotions become anger. This is a problem. It's a problem for men. It's a problem for women. It's a problem for non-binary folks. Everyone is hurt by this patriarchal nonsense. The other piece of this is like we alluded to, we're talking about heart attacks, is that men have different symptoms and anxiety presents differently. Now, there's no way of knowing right now, if that is because of biology or because of culture. In reality, it's probably both.

One of the things that I see far more often in men with anxiety is the presentation of exercise intolerance. Now, this is a known symptom of anxiety, but it's not one that we talk about a lot. Sometimes the only way that anxiety gets diagnosed, is this inability to exercise and respiratory symptoms that are the signs of an anxiety attack.

I've met men that have this any time they exercise and I've met men that have these symptoms, only during specific exercises. It's not that women can't have exercise intolerance when they have anxiety because some of them do. But I have found at least in my clinical experience for this to be more frequent in men.

The other area, I see more men seeking help, at least for anxiety is when it upsets their digestive system. We know that this happens in women as well, and I see plenty of women with IBS and anxiety. But more men in my office have digestive disturbances as their main symptom than women.

Closing the gap

If we are ever going to reduce collective anxiety, we're going to have to break this gap in diagnosis. We need a culture where everyone is allowed to express their feelings, where we don't assume that racing thoughts or worry is the cornerstone of an anxiety diagnosis and when we do away with harmful sterotypes and language like "man up" that allows each of us to enjoy the emotional freedom and recieve the support they deserve.

My wish for you is that you find the place where you can identify and express the full range of human emotions. We all have the right to each of our feelings. In order to live in a place of congruence where we're connected to ourselves, where we are not in a place of internal stress and anxiety, it's really important to identify our true emotions.

Chapter Twenty
CATCH AND RELEASE (FOR FEELINGS)

IT WAS MID-MARCH, AND I WAS WALKING INTO MY OFFICE ON A FRIDAY morning with this deep feeling like this was going to be the last time I was in my office for a while. The news cycle was picking up around this new virus called SARS-CoV-2 and the COVID-19 disease it causes. I could feel the overwhelm building.

It was a combination of not knowing what was coming—not really knowing how to prepare. Even in my limited knowledge of what to prepare, not being sure what the next steps were supposed to be. And also just the number of steps. There were so many things, all needing to get done immediately. It was almost paralyzing.

One of the things I have learned about overwhelm is that it's not your to-do list. It's the feelings underneath the to-do list that create the overwhelm. So I walked myself through a process that I call "catch and release."

I teach this to all of my patients through the tranquil minds program for handling overwhelm. We're much more effective at solving problems when we're acting from a state of being centred, rather than reacting.

This works in our personal life as well.

How many times have you argued with your spouse over who's supposed to be doing the dishes? We all know. It's not really about the dishes. But it's impossible to sort through who should be washing them if underneath you're actually just angry or scared or hurt.

Catching your feelings

The first step of the catch and release - the catching part - is to name your feelings. Imagine a pond full of fish, and each fish is a different emotion. Some are sadness. One might say: fear, overwhelm, happiness, rage, jealousy, joy, contentment. All of these fish are swimming in the pool. The first step is to go in with your net and catch the fish that names the feeling that you are having right now.

When an emotion presents, start with just naming it: happy, sad, mad, joyful, afraid etc. When you get that general category, for example, mad, you could then go in deeper and ask yourself, "is this irritation? Am I frustrated? Am I angry? Or am I Enraged?" The more clearly you can define your feeling, the more easily you can process it and move through each feeling without it disrupting your core.

If you find you always go into one emotion, that's an opportunity to look at whether you've been socialized into that emotion. Perhaps there is something else happening. The important thing is just to be curious.

Taking the time to identify the complex layers of emotions that you have underneath your current situation, helps reduce the overwhelm. By naming something you can see it. So rather than an overwhelming mess of mushy undefined emotions swirling inside you. There's this clarity of, "Yeah, I'm actually mad about this, but I'm also feeling quite pleased about this other piece. And I'm a little worried because I don't want this to become that."

When you start putting them all out there, you're like, no wonder I'm overwhelmed! That's a lot to be happening at once, but I hadn't even acknowledged all these different pieces. Now, once you've named these feelings and caught these fish, the next thing to do is let them go.

This is not a "catch and keep" type of situation. This is catch and release. You don't need to be carrying the fish of anger in your backpack all day - it will start to smell. You need to put it back into the pond until you need it again.

Releasing your feelings

How do we release these feelings? There's a couple of different ways that I walk my patients through. And I'm going to share all of these with you now. Some of them will work better for you or for different feelings. And you may need to play around to find out what lets these feelings get back out.

Not all of these are things you're able to do as soon as you notice a feeling. Obviously, if your boss pisses you off in a meeting, you can't just be like, "Oh, hey, I'm going to go for a run right now. Let's finish our chat later! Bye!" It's still important to identify that feeling "oh I'm pissed off" and release the feeling, say by going for the run, but you may not be able to do it right away. That's okay. But you must do it.

This helps build connection with yourself. After you've identified the emotion, it needs to go somewhere. If you just shove it down, the feeling is just going to sit in your body and pop up someplace else. I don't know if you've ever had the experience of thinking, "this is an inopportune time to cry, so I'm just not going to be sad" and then having it pop up at another time! If you aren't careful, it's not necessarily a better time!

Our emotions are real, they are made of molecules, and they stay in our bodies where they interact with all our bodily systems. If the feelings are not getting expressed, then they just stay in our bodies. It's really important that we let them out.

So let's get into how we can release emotions.

Words

Using words is a great way to let feelings go. Even just by naming and acknowledging the feelings may be enough to let some lighter feelings be processed and free. Saying, "Wow, that's really irritating" is sometimes enough to take the edge off that irritation and allow you to move forward and not have it follow with you through the day. Sometimes, acknowledging that just for yourself is enough. Other times we need to let it out. That's why sharing words can be helpful. Sometimes it's appropriate to address the source of your emotions directly. Maybe you're at work, and the person behind or beside you has started humming. And it's irritating you, and you turn around you say, "Hey, can you knock that off - that humming is really distracting me right now." And the hummer is like, "Yeah, no problem, I didn't realize I was doing it." You've used your words to identify your feeling and express it. Problem solved. Hopefully, you're not feeling irritated anymore.

Sometimes that's not the most appropriate way to deal with things in terms of expression. If you can't express yourself to the irritating person, perhaps you don't know this person, personally, or you have no access to them. An example would be political frustration, where you're annoyed by something. A member of Parliament or you're pissed off at the president of the United States. Well, you can't just turn to him and say, "Look, you shouldn't have said that, that's really annoying me," but words can still be helpful in this kind of situation to process the feeling. You may turn to a friend or partner and say, "can you believe what that guy just said." And sometimes that's enough.

You also can use writing, either to yourself or to someone else, to let go of feelings. To do this, you might write a letter. You might write a letter to a politician or to the public figure that's pissed you off or maybe a tweet and say, "you know, that's BS don't do that." and saying that kind of thing. It helps process the anger and let it out. A lot of people use Twitter for this. It's their release valve. It's important to make sure that it actually is letting things go, and then you're not getting in a cycle of increasing rage and frustration. A lot of people get stuck in that on Twitter too. I am just saying.

The other way to express things in words is to keep it to yourself. I know, maybe that's not super popular in 2020, we all like to have our voices heard myself included. Still, there's nothing wrong with just keeping a journal and writing, this pissed me off today, or this made me really sad or scared or uncomfortable or joyful, or whatever it is. Any of the feelings fish that you've caught; all of those feelings can be written out. In that way, that fish can be let back into the pond.

Creativity
Creative pursuits are another way to let go of feelings. By engaging in that feeling through a creative means, you can then begin to process it and let it go. Many people make art. Write poetry. Paint. Draw. Build—any kind of creation to process a feeling. But you don't have to be the creator to use creativity as a way to process your feelings. You can also just enjoy something someone else has created. Dive into that piece of media and feel those feelings.

Let's say you're missing your friend, and you're feeling sad. Once you've named that feeling as sadness, you may choose to process it by watching a sad movie, listening to sad music, anything that helps you emote to feel that feeling completely so that it's not stuck in your body and it's not staying with you. It just, it just leaves. This way it doesn't matter whether you're actually getting out your guitar and playing that music, or if you're just throwing on a song that makes you feel that way. It's the engagement in the collective emotion that is brought out through the art that helps let it go.

Physical Activity
The last we're going to talk about processing your emotions is through physical activity, which I alluded to earlier. Because emotions live as molecules in our body, processing

them through physical activity is a reasonable method. This is innate; you can see animals do this as they shake out their fear. And we can do this as well, we can take our rage, our sorrow, our fear and our frustration and we can channel it through movement.

When I was at the Canadian College of Naturopathic Medicine, I had a supervisor, and he used to make fun of runners playfully. He told us, anytime you've got someone that's a runner, you should look at them and say, "what are running from." It was just like this little joking way of saying that anybody who's THAT into running is avoiding something. Personally, I don't think he's spot on. I think anybody that's running that much is processing something.

This is in the same way that any of our habits are a form of processing. Certainly, movement is that healthier choice than drinking too much beer or pretending that you do not actually have any feelings.

Think of exercise as a release valve for your emotions—another way to get that fish back into the water. Run. Kickbox. Lift. Do yoga, whatever it takes to transform that feeling so that it's no longer stuck in you.

Once you've let your feeling go, then you can solve the problem.

Everyone wants to jump to this part. There's a tendency to think that solving the problem will solve your feelings. But there are two separate issues, and you're more effective at problem-solving when you're not exploding with unexpressed rage.

Ask yourself, "what's a healthy way for me to express this particular emotion" Most importantly, this is about creating space for any emotion. When you create space for every feeling, you are not ruled by any of them because every feeling is okay. None of the feelings are overwhelming.

When I think back to the beginning of this pandemic, I am thinking about all the steps I needed to take and all the things I needed to do. There was no way to move through those steps until I took a moment to acknowledge the fear and the grief that we were all experiencing. I had to process those feelings. It was impossible to make rational choices that were going to move my life forward.

Take Action ✏️

Think of a time when you were feeling overwhelmed, or use this activity the next time you feel overwhelmed. Write down a list of all of your feelings related to what you're feeling overwhelmed by. Also, write down anything you feel in that moment related to your life and circumstance. Then let those feelings go. Create, talk about it, write it down, listen to music, move your body, do whatever it takes, so that those feelings are fully expressed and no longer stuck in your body.

Chapter Twenty One
COMMUNITY

ONE OF MY FAVOURITE PODCASTERS IS MIKE MACCARUGH, WHO GOES BY "Science Mike."[22] He is always reminding me of our human need for community connection as he repeats, "We are social primates." I love this reminder because it reinforces the idea that we are not meant to be alone. Needing other humans is not a personality trait or a defect but that our biology, our neural wiring, it's all set up this way. We are meant to be part of a community. We don't need to be cool. We don't need to be aloof. We need to be here, present and connected with other humans.

So much of this book has been dedicated to what might be reasonably referred to as "self-care." However, what we really need is community care. Because when shit hits the fan, yes, we want to be in the most resilient place that we can be for ourselves. But what really helps us survive and thrive in these times is when our community shows up.

In 2007, my brother was in a car accident. In the aftermath, our community appeared. Our community showed up for us in cards and prayers, in snacks at the hospital, and in more Christmas presents that I have ever received one Christmas. They showed up in the meals which arrived at my parents' house several nights a week. When my parents were at the hospital, my sister had friends who let her stay over at their house, who made her breakfast and made sure she got off to school in the morning. They showed up on our driveway - where my dad never shovelled once that winter. All of this happened because our community showed up for us.

What makes up a community

Your community is made of your friends. Friends are the people in your life who give a damn. They actually care about your life, and they genuinely want to celebrate you. Friends don't just exist in isolation; you can also cultivate friendship in groups. Things like sports teams, religious organizations, committees, clubs can create your community. Any place where you show up and connect to people.

At this point, you are probably in one of two places. Either you feel like you have a strong community and you have a lot of friends, or you know that you need more community and more friends.

Start with what you have

Either way, start by loving the friends you have. Call them. Text them. Start practicing showing up for them in real practical, tangible ways. If you can, drive their kids to soccer practice when yours are going too. Drop off a casserole. Shovel the walkway if someone's in the hospital. Be there in any way you can, practically and emotionally, with a listening ear. This is how you build stronger bonds with the people that you already know and love. It's good for your relationship with them, but it's also good for you because that form of connection reminds you that you're not in this alone, that you have other people and doing good for others is good soul food.

You might need more friends

Now, you might feel that you need more community. If you think, "wow, I actually need more friends," you should know that you're not alone." I know that it feels very lonely, but I want you to know the good news. There are lots of other people just like you who are looking for more friends in their life. In a world of technology, where we feel more connected than ever before, we're actually more disconnected and spend less and less time actually hanging out with other people. This is problematic for us social primates. So, if you are in a position where you feel like you need more community, I want you to know that you can build it.

I'm going to tell you about my 30th birthday. I'd been living in my current city for almost four years. I had a two-year-old. I wanted to have a party, and I thought, "who can I invite?" Yes, I had friends that live in other cities, but I felt like I didn't have a big community in my own city. I went back to work when my daughter was three months old. I didn't have "mom friends," and I desperately wanted more people to call at a moment's notice to come over for dinner or meet up for a coffee or just talk!

So right then, I set an intention that I was going to make more friends. Then I started to show up for that. I got involved. I called people back. I made plans, and I created time in my schedule to follow up with people. A year later, I could confidently say I'd made many new friendships, people I love and can't imagine my life without. Also, I had spent more time with my existing friends that I had previously felt so disconnected from.

So, how did I do that?

The first thing is I got vulnerable. I acknowledged that I wanted more friends and that I was going to have to put myself in situations to make them.

Meeting People At Community or Networking Events

It's really easy when you're in a group of people, especially if you have a bit of social anxiety, to just not talk to anyone and get your phone out. This is not going to help you build connections and community. Avoid the corner when you're in social situations. Find someone to introduce yourself to ask their name, and ask them lots of questions about their life. Find out what you have in common with them. Think about what event you are at - you both came to it so there will be some kind of connection there!

If you can't find someone to talk to - stand alone if there is a bistro table - stand there. I know it's scary, but it works! Take an open posture and smile. Don't look at your phone. Sip some water and - wait. I can't tell you how many networking events I've been at, or parties where I've known not a soul and just by standing at a table by myself and putting a smile on my face, someone else who is desperately looking not to stand alone will come over and approach me. The next thing you know, that little table is the hub of the party.

Creating Community

The next thing that you want to do is make sure to schedule things. Commit to spending more time with people. Try setting up recurring events. Maybe that's a sports team or a regular club like a book club, but it can also just be a group of people or one other person that you get together with regularly. When something happens at the same time, for example, Saturday brunch, then it becomes a standard plan. You don't have to reach out, and it doesn't take as much effort. If you've got five friends you go for brunch with every week, then everyone assumes you're having brunch.

When you don't have a standard plan, plan your next meet up at the one that you're currently having. So if you're having coffee with a new friend or if you've invited old friends out to dinner, listen for when someone says, "This is fun. We should do it again." That's your cue. When they do get out your phone and say, "I'd love to. Let's schedule it!" Yes, there is some risk, maybe someone will laugh, but you and your friends are busy people and most of the time someone thinks it's a great idea! This helps build continuity in your friendships and continue to build that continuity.

Take Action ✏️

Call a friend you haven't spoken to in longer than you'd wish. Don't overthink it. As long as it's not the middle of the night where you are calling, it's fine to call someone and say, "I was just thinking of you! How are you doing? Do you have some time to chat?"

Chapter Twenty Two
CONNECTING TO SOMETHING BIGGER

I FEEL LIKE I'M TRYING TO FIT A CHAPTER ABOUT EXISTENTIAL ANXIETY AT THE end of this book, but I have this theory I can't leave alone. Some of this anxiety epidemic we are in right now is a spiritual crisis.

Look, I don't care what your religious or spiritual beliefs are. It doesn't matter to me if you believe in God, look for signs from the universe, meet the divine in nature or are a staunch atheist (yes, multiple categories may apply.) What matters is that we create some space to acknowledge that there are some types of anxiety that are soothed by getting out of our heads and connecting—connecting not just to other people, but to something bigger.

God. The universe. Collective consciousness. Love.

The idea that we are alone, that none of this stuff matters, can be paralyzing. I'm not saying I have any answers here. I'm saying that the exploration of these questions is sacred.This is the work of reaching out and connecting, even if you never hear back. Even for questions that we cannot know the answers to. To pretend this does not influence our experience of anxiety would be a lie.

Like passion, love is a feeling that overrides anxiety, when we fill ourselves with love and compassion and when we understand that we are all interconnected. There is a deep level of anxiety caused by isolation that dissipates when we connect with this.

Connecting to Awe and Wonder

How do we cultivate that sense of connectedness? The first place is to consider wonder and awe. When was the last time you felt wonder? When were you last struck with the awesomeness that exists in this world?

I ask this question to a lot of people, and there are a lot of different answers out there.

The most recurrent theme I hear back is people telling me about the time spent in nature. Surprisingly, even people who don't really like nature or don't consider themselves "outdoorsy" often fall back to the natural environment when they stop and think. Nature is a beautiful source of wonder in our world. It's full of sunsets and sunrises, snowfalls and waterfalls, streams and oceans, mountains, prairies and forests. It is profound and beautiful. Through its expansiveness and its beauty, it connects us all and connects us to that sensation of awe.

In addition to cultivating awe and wonder, being in nature is just straight up good for you. It reduces stress. It's good for your attention and your mental health. If you aren't sure what next step to take from this section - spend more time in nature[23].

The second most common answer I hear is on the theme of art. When was the last time that you interacted with an art form that you thought was just really amazing and awesome? Maybe it was a piece of music, a movie, or a book. It might have been a building or even the design of a household object. Any of these things can have a certain beauty, or intelligence to them, or even a story that we can connect to. When we connect to an object and see the humanity behind it, we see the humanity in the maker. We see our humanity in that as well, and it creates a bridge of connection. That connection leads us toward oneness and love.

We are all connected. Whatever we do for others, we do for ourselves and for everyone. When we isolate, and we allow fears of separation, fears of judgment and anxiety to keep us from connecting, it doesn't just hurt us. It hurts everyone. Our partners, our families, our workplaces and our communities need to connect.

If you're not sure where to start with all this, start by spending some time feeling wonder. It doesn't have to be complicated. Go outside, hang out with some trees, watch a movie or listen to some music, and give it your full attention. Connect with that sensation of awe that sensation of wonder and cultivate that feeling of expansiveness, because this expansiveness has a way of driving out fear.

Creating a Gratitude Practice

Another way to cultivate more appreciation and awareness for the goodness in your life is to create a gratitude list. One of the ways that this works is by activating a particular part in your brain called the reticular activating center or RAS. And what this part of your brain does is it looks for what's important. It's really the filter in your concious mind, and it picks up your sensory information that your body is experiencing and chooses what to share with your conscious mind. It determines which pieces are important and moves them up to the level of your consciousness. If you tried to proccess your entire surroundings you would be overwhelmed. The classic example to understand the reticular activating center is when you think about buying a new car.

Have you ever noticed that when you choose a new car, or you start thinking about buying a specific new car, all of a sudden you see it everywhere? Somehow, you are surrounded by that exact car, and you're wondering, "how come all my neighbours just got this car?" They didn't just get this car. It's that your brain now sends the information about that car up to your conscious mind. Your reticular activating center has awoken to these cars. It is saying this is now important information.

We tend as humans to focus on the negative, to keep ourselves safe we look for risk. But we can train ourselves to look for the good, the positive, and the joy. One of the ways we do this is through the same brain structures that allow us to find all of the new cars. This is the structure where we are paying attention and tuned in to the good in our lives. And we use gratitude to cultivate that. Gratitude practices don't have to be complicated. They don't have to look the same way your parents or grandparents practiced gratitude. If you want to say prayers before you eat or before you sleep, and that's your gratitude practice, that's great, and you should do that. But if that's not your style, don't feel like that's the only way to be grateful. Maybe you want to keep a gratitude list where you take some time every day to write down a few things that you're grateful for. You might want to do this in a phone app, a paper journal, or on top of your daily calendar. You may want to say it out loud to yourself before you go to sleep or share with your family as part of bedtime or mealtime or as a way to get your day started. It doesn't really matter how you do it. Increasing your conscious awareness of goodness in your life will help you find more goodness.

Starting with what you feel grateful for

When you make a gratitude list, you want to include the things that you're thankful for. Some of these things can be big or repetitive, and there are a few ways to think of what you're grateful for. They're the obvious ones. Maybe you're grateful for your health, your home, the safety of your community, or the country you live in. You might be grateful that you have access to running water and food in your fridge. These are all great things to be grateful for, but they are not the only way that you can focus on gratitude. You can also focus on the small things, the specific things that bring joy to your day. Maybe a really warm cup of coffee. Maybe you're grateful for the smell of your shampoo. The more stress you're under, the more I recommend focusing on the small things, which can be easier to see.

Creating a gratitude chain

When things feel like they're not really going your way, the next thing you can do to expand your gratitude list is to create a gratitude chain. This is an exercise where you start with something that you're grateful for. And then you expand it, building a chain to include more and more people and things you are thankful for. We'll go back to the example of that cup of coffee. If you're grateful for that Friday morning coffee, which I always am, then you can also be thankful for the barista that made the coffee. You can be thankful for the delivery truck driver that drove the coffee beans from the roaster to the coffee shop. You can be thankful for the coffee roasters that took those beautiful beans and processed them into this wonderful thing called coffee. You can be thankful for the people that grew the coffee and put their love and their energy into this plant to create your cup of coffee. You can continue in this manner thinking of anyone that shipped the coffee people that made the permits to allow the coffee to cross borders. People that made the cars and the airplanes that flew the coffee to you. Soon, you realize that hundreds of people are involved in you enjoying this cup of coffee. We then expand this gratitude from a small, focussed joy at your morning coffee to include all the people who made all the ingredients that went into this cup of coffee. That's a lot of gratitude out in the world.

Finding gratitude in challenges

The other way you can grow your gratitude list is by looking at the challenging things and finding the gift. I know some things suck. And maybe you don't want to look for a gift in them. That's your right. I don't know your trauma. I don't know your story. I don't know how safe it is for you to look for gratitude in something that's very difficult. But you deserve to know that it's an option, even if it's a big problem. So if this is accessible to you, and you want to give it a try, you can take something difficult and find gratitude in it. Maybe you don't have gratitude for the full experience, which might require Herculean effort. And that's okay if it's just not there. But maybe you can find a bit of gratitude for something that came out of it.

Let's take a small inconvenience, like a traffic jam that made you late for work. Maybe you had to be rerouted, and you went a different way. Maybe while taking that way, you went over a bridge, and the bridge was unexpectedly pretty. Maybe you can find some gratitude for getting to see that beautiful bridge today, even if you're annoyed about the overall situation.

I would definitely recommend practicing with those minor inconveniences and frustrations rather than pulling up your deepest, darkest challenges and trying to find the gratitude in them. Although, to be honest, that can be quite healing as well.

However you choose to build your gratitude list, the important thing is to do it consistently. Don't build a gratitude list once, and then never look at it or never add to it. This is a practice, not an activity. Think of incorporating a moment of gratitude every day.

Take Action ✎

Create a gratitude list. Find a time to review it, add to it, or make a new one everyday as part of your routine.

Chapter Twenty Three
YOU CAN CREATE CALM FROM THE INSIDE OUT

YOU'VE REACHED THE END OF THE TRANQUIL MINDS METHOD AND TO CLOSE I want to share with you my why behind this book and why I'm so passionate about sharing this information

In my first chapter, I gave my big Goal for Create Calm - I honestly believe you can create a life of calm moments, from the inside out, no matter what is going on in your life. Now I want you to know why I'm so passionate about teaching this information and sharing the secrets to more peaceful moments to as many people as possible.

When I was 6 years old I missed a ton of school because of tummy aches. My stomach would hurt out of nowhere. I would cry and have to go home from school. My parents were worried. My doctors were worried. I had to do all kinds of tests, including one where I had to drink this thick liquid, wear a paper gown, and lay on a cold metal table for what felt like forever. They found nothing, because the problem wasn't physically in my stomach, in spite of the very real physical pain. I didn't know it then, but I realize now, this was my first experience of anxiety.

When I was 22 years old I started studying naturopathic medicine. The hours were long, the classes were challenging, and I felt like I was living in a pressure cooker. Exams came every six weeks, whether I needed them or not. Eventually, this state of stress turned into something a little more sinister.

At first, I felt like I could never "calm down" I started crying over almost everything. My walk to and from campus became a terrifying part of my day, where I kept checking over my shoulder, afraid that someone was going to jump at me and attack. NOT. NORMAL. Oh, and those stomach aches I told you about? Well, they came back in full force, and no kind of "clean eating" could make things feel "normal" again.

I knew I needed to do something differently. So slowly, I started taking the techniques I was studying and testing them out on myself. I changed how I was eating. I started getting acupuncture. I tried yoga for the first time. I tried A LOT of different supplements, running my own experiments on what worked for me in which types of situations.

In 2014 I started seeing patients. As it turns out, I wasn't the only one out there to have struggled with an anxiety disorder or struggled to manage a stressful situation. I quickly found I loved working with patients who were feeling stressed, overwhelmed or anxious. I loved learning what was working (and not working) for my patients.

As I worked longer in the mental health field, I saw similar patterns emerge in my patients and in the research. I became obsessed with my patients' blood sugar and making sure that was well regulated. Same with their sleep. And stress levels. And I felt like a broken record.

Did I tell you about blood sugar? Oh, OK, right. How's your sleep? Still bad? But we talked about sleep hygiene. Oh, we ran out of time. Yes, let's do that today.

There were these five key areas that I needed to address with ALL my patients. These were things that could either be creating calm in their lives OR totally undermining all the work we were doing with acupuncture and supplements. In fact, left unchecked, these things were actually creating stress and anxiety!

I knew I needed to put these five pillars into a system, to make sure each person had all the information and support they needed to OPTIMIZE each of these behaviours so they were creating the environment for calm to support whatever other interventions they were using.

And that is how the Tranquil Minds Program was born.

My mission is to help as many people as I can to create calm in their lives so they can do the work they are here to do. I want to reduce the amount of anxiety the world feels, and share this methodology with as many people as possible. I know you can create a calm and meaningful life from the inside out.

What are you doing to bring yourself peace and clarity from focusing on what really matters in your life? Are you doing everything in your power to create the change in this world that only you can contribute? You can create calm from the inside out. This is the driving force behind the book and my work, and it's contagious. When you are calm it creates calm in people around you.

I had a patient, let's call them Corey, who was missing work due to their anxiety.

You see, Corey's stress affected their digestive system. When they were worried or anxious, they just had to go (you know what I mean?) This made travel difficult, even just commuting for work was challenging in the mornings.

With Corey, we focused - yes on the digestive system - but also on stress and anxiety management through the five pillars of the Tranquil Minds Program. With a few simple changes to Corey's diet, their anxiety symptoms were so well managed they were able to stop missing work.

When IBS is triggered by stress, it's life-changing to have it under control. But Corey, like most of you, didn't want their health better just to have better health or even to be a more productive and reliable worker, although this is important. It's the bigger changes that come with the increased confidence from better managing your physical and mental health that get me out of bed in the morning. After this, Corey used their new confidence to propose to their partner. It's stuff like this that makes my heart melt.

Here's the best part - you can do the same thing. You can have peace of mind. Cope through whatever life throws at you without losing your cool or acting in a way that's incongruent with your values. Live a life of authenticity that leaves you proud of your legacy.

Yes, it takes work. There will be time and effort involved in this. It doesn't happen by magic. But this time and effort can change your work, your relationships, and how you see yourself.

With the Tranquil Minds Method, your life will start to change in ways you can imagine and probably also in ways you haven't even considered yet.

Yes you might have to

→ miss out on some late nights
→ get up early even on the weekend
→ have some hard conversations
→ convince yourself to keep trying when you fail
→ risk being wrong sometimes
→ put yourself at the top of your priority list

In the end, all this is worth it when you are able to contribute more fully to your life because you are not being held back by your anxiety.

Why I wrote this book

I wrote this book because I wanted to share this methodology with anyone who wanted to learn about it. I want to make a difference in your life and the life of your company, family and community. I want to share the peace that has been given to me with you.

I want you to have a life that is authentically yours.

I want you to wake up in the morning full of excitement and without dread for your day.

I want you to know yourself, to see yourself and be seen as yourself in everything you do.

I hope your self-care turns into self-love - the kind that radiates towards every person you meet, giving them permission to love themselves too.

I want your family, friends and community to be transformed by the steady, grounded presence you create in any space you enter.

I want you to be free from making decisions based on fear and move into decisions based on joy.

I know you can do this. I have witnessed many others do by following the Tranquil Minds Method that I have laid out for you in this book.

The key is to take action. Commit to yourself that you will improve your health and your mindset.

You picked up this book for a reason. It sparked your interest because you, too, want a world with more joy, more peace and more calm.

It's yours.

You just have to walk through it.

Tranquil Minds Program: My Bigger Mission

While a lot of my time is spent working with patients as their naturopathic doctor and guiding them through this transformation, I knew that being a clinician, I could only help so many people that way. Anxiety is an epidemic in North America, and I can only take on so many patients.

I created the Tranquil Minds Online Program to help even more people in overcoming anxiety. I knew that some of what my patients were doing (like getting more sleep and eating vegetables), could be done without my supervision. I want to empower as many people as possible with the education they need to make the changes sustainably and systematically such that they can create more calm for themselves.

The Mission of the Tranquil Minds Program is to create a more peaceful world, one person at a time from the inside out.

If you want more calm in your life and you think you might want the extra support of the Tranquil Minds Program, I encourage you to check it out. It is the next level of support for anyone who needs more than a book to change their life and their habits.

Check it out here: https://katiethomsonaitken.com/tranquil-minds/

Regardless of whether or not you want to join the Tranquil Minds Program, I want to hear your success stories!

I hope you will send me a note when you've worked through this book telling me how you are doing had how your life has changed.

You can reach me at drkatie@tranquilmindnaturopath.com

Here's to you creating calm,

Dr. Katie

Tranquil Minds

Now It's Your Turn

Access the guided methodology to create calm in your life in only 6 weeks.

Even if you are busy, stressed out and don't know where you are starting from, you can build healthy habits that reduce anxiety and set you up for a lifetime of health and wellbeing.

The Tranquil Minds Program is the educational course for professionals working to overcome anxiety from the comfort of home.

DON'T WAIT

Register for the Tranquil Minds Program Today:
www.katiethomsonaitken.com/tranquil-minds

Can you help me?

Thank You For Reading My Book!

I appreciate all of your feedback and would love to know what you thought of this book.

I need your feedback to make the next version of this book, and my future books and programs better.

Please leave me a helpful review on Amazon and let me know what you thought of the book.

Thank you!

~ Dr. Katie

ACKNOWLEDGEMENTS

This book would not be in your hands (or on your screen) without the love and support of so many people in my life.

Thank you to my husband who supports me endlessly. When I said I wanted to go all in on writing this book he was nothing but encouraging with his words, his actions and his permission to share about him and us in this book. Thank you Joel.

To my daughter, I know you might not understand why mommy was always working on her book but I hope that when you get older you use your incredible determination to go after whatever dreams you have in your own life.

Thank you to my editor Ben Robinson who pushed me to turn this book from a small DIY guide into something much more personal. Everything that makes me uncomfortable about this book is here because you.

To my sister-in-law Sarah who took my word document and turned it into the beautifully formatted book in your hands. I assure you the final version would lack much of this finesse without her gracious eye for detail.

Thank you to Dr. Anne Hussain ND for helping me see my blind spots in this text. I'm so grateful for your support and your friendship.

To Sarah Wilson, who showed up and stepped in exactly when I needed more help with enthusiasm and dedication. Thank you for your leadership.

Thank you to my entire launch team; to everyone who read the book in advance and supported me and this book - your support means the world to me. I couldn't have done this without you.

To my patients, thank you for sharing your health, concerns, and experiences with me. So much of this book is grounded it what I have learned from you

Finally, thank you to you for reading this book and joining in on my mission to create a calmer and more peaceful world.

About the Author

Dr. Katie Thomson Aitken ND, is a mental health wellness advocate, author of Create Calm and founder of the Tranquil Minds Program for professionals with anxiety. Katie believes that when times get tough, heading back to basics is the most powerful thing we can do for our health. When away from her practice, Katie spends her time cooking and singing Diseny songs on demand for her daughter.

www. tranquilmindnaturopath.com

Made in the USA
Middletown, DE
18 October 2020